AUTHENTIC LOVE

DISCOVER THE DEEP TRUE LOVE YOU DESERVE

KIMBERLEY ARNOLD

KWE PUBLISHING

To Conner, my son, who came to this world to help me awaken my Authentic Love and whose heart, soul, and wisdom shines through, blessing and benefiting this world.

To Lama Lhanang Rinpoche, for his wisdom, compassion, and teachings, which awakened in me the fundamentals of Authentic Love and guided me on my path.

CONTENTS

INTRODUCTION

Amor est vitae essentia.
(Love is the essence of life.)
—Unknown

WHAT IS the best you have ever felt? Have you ever experienced a time when you felt content, at peace, and with a feeling of lacking nothing? For me, this occurred when my newborn son was placed on my chest, when I received a hug from my spiritual teacher, at times during the first few weeks of a new love, and during meditation. For many, this has also occurred when in the presence of a grandparent or grandchild, just before death, or during a marriage ceremony. These are all examples of feeling Authentic Love. It is possible to experience this feeling more consistently and on a greater scale.

For others, they may never have experienced Authentic Love. The feeling of an absence of Authentic Love can be more prevalent than a feeling of having Authentic Love. This absence of Authentic Love can feel like something is missing in your life or in your relationships—a deep-seated emotion that felt like you had a hole in your heart. Were you neglected as child, which continues to trouble you? Do you go from relationship to relationship looking for love, only to find that the love disappears or does not measure up? These are all symptoms of the effects of a lack of Authentic Love in your life.

Authentic Love is not the same as "love," which is used under many circumstances in our modern Western society. The definition of "love" in the *Merriam-Webster Dictionary* includes eight separate definitions (not including "a score of zero in tennis"!). It describes numerous aspects of love, including sexual love, nonsexual love, and simple affection. One of the many problems with discussing and teaching love is the confusion related to what love actually means. Love, it turns out, appears to be extremely subjective. How can we carry on with using one word—love—when it has so many different meanings?

This book seeks to explain a concept that I identify as "Authentic Love." I'll talk about why our very existence depends on it, how it affects our lives, why we need to educate people and children about Authentic Love, and why we need to make Authentic Love a conventional word and a mainstream topic. This book provides information supported by science, religions and belief systems, great spiritual masters, and ordinary, actually extraordinary, people. Note that while none of these people, organizations, or ideologies actually use the term "Authentic Love", it is clear by their description and explanation of a deeper form of love that they mean Authentic Love, by my description.

I will show you what Authentic Love is and how to recognize it, but more importantly how to generate it. Yes, it can and should be taught, which is why we need to understand and bring this concept into conventional society and teach Authentic Love in schools. In schools, we teach children about sex, anger, greed, pride, and every other emotion that humans experience. We do teach about love, but because the concept of love is not well defined or understood by adults, the result is immense confusion. Ask any child or adult what love is, and each will give you a different explanation. When Authentic Love is grasped, it makes the world of difference in anyone's, let alone a child's, life.

Throughout this book, I describe and explain Authentic Love as a noun, a verb, a feeling, a consciousness, a process, and a path. It is indeed all of these things. Similar to the word *love*, Authentic Love is a noun, as it is a thing and a subject. Authentic Love is an action as it is expressed as a feeling. As you will see, Authentic Love is a state of being or consciousness that can ultimately be permanent but until that time is typically intermittent. Authentic Love is also a spiritual process or path that leads you to who you are, your soul, and connects you to the Divine or God or universal consciousness, which results in joy, peace, and contentment.

> **Authentic Love is the process
> of leading you back to yourself,
> who you really are.**

1. WHAT IS AUTHENTIC LOVE?

Love is real, real is love.
—"Love" by John Lennon

WHAT IS AUTHENTIC LOVE? It is what is left when your ego disappears, fades into the background, or withdraws. It brings you joy, contentment, and peace. It makes others feel beautiful and worthy. Without it, you feel depression and pain. Authentic Love is needed for our very survival and quality of life. It is the essence of our existence, which is supported by science, religion, and ancient and modern-day spiritual masters.

Religions, spiritual belief systems and spiritual masters all teach that Authentic Love is within us; it is our real true self. The purpose of our lives is to grow into Authentic Love. We

> Love is an open secret, the most obvious thing in the world and the most hidden, with no why to how it keeps its mystery.
>
> — Rumi

just need to peel back what is surrounding it and realize that we are Authentic Love. Marianne Williamson in *A Return to Love* writes, "Love is our ultimate reality and our purpose on earth" (Williamson, 1996). She further states that the experience of love is the meaning of life and that "love is the essential existential fact" (Williamson, 1996).

We are all born with Authentic Love and the ability to generate it. Throughout our emotional and physical development, we typically learn fear. We learn what not to do for fear of the consequences. Our life's journey is to unlearn fear and relearn Authentic Love.

Sometimes in order to understand a concept, it is helpful to know what it is *not*. Generally, Authentic Love is not a romantic notion or a love with conditions or expectations. Authentic Love cannot exist with negative emotions, such as jealousy, anger, selfishness, or superiority. It is not flippant or frivolous. Authentic Love is also not that uncomfortable feeling of desperation when you love someone so much that you would die without them. It does not make your heart hurt or your stomach ache.

Authentic Love is the thought of loving someone even if they don't love you back. Authentic Love is the feeling when your heart opens and your ego ceases to exist or fades even for a few moments, as the ego with all of its selfish wants, desires, and stories cannot exist in the light of Authentic Love. What is left is the soul, the true you, which is Authentic Love.

Definition of Authentic Love

First, we need to be clear about how we have used the word *love*. We have used this word under countless circumstances to mean so many things, for numerous reasons. While the word *love* has resulted in immense joy and innumerable benefits, the use and misuse of the word has also led to misunderstanding and confusion. Before we go any further, let me ask you the following questions: How do you define love? Is it the feeling between two people that is sexual in nature, or can it be in a platonic relationship? Is it the feeling you get when you hold a baby in your arms or when you see that amazing large-screen television or the designer purse you want to buy?

According to *Merriam-Webster's Dictionary*, it is all of the above and more:

1. a (1): strong affection for another arising out of kinship or personal ties (e.g., maternal love for a child); (2) attraction based on sexual desire: affection and tenderness felt by lovers; (3) affection based on admiration, benevolence, or common interests (e.g., love for his old schoolmates);

b: an assurance of affection (e.g., give her my love)

2. warm attachment, enthusiasm, or devotion (e.g., love of the sea)

3. a: the object of attachment, devotion, or admiration (e.g., baseball was his first love);

b (1): a beloved person: darling—often used as a term of endearment; (2) British—used as an informal term of address

4. a: unselfish loyal and benevolent concern for the good of another: as (1) the fatherly concern of God for humankind, or (2) brotherly concern for others;

b: a person's adoration of God

5. a god or personification of love

6. an amorous episode: love affair

7. the sexual embrace: copulation

8. a score of zero (as in tennis)

9. capitalized Christian Science: God

How can we have effective, meaningful, clear discussions or express how we feel when there are at least eight definitions (not including the tennis reference as I think we can remove that definition in this case) of the word *love*? Is it any wonder why people are always so confused about love?

When someone says the word *love* in conversation, it

usually means a type of romantic affection or the love of an object, such as a house, jewelry, or pizza. When someone says, "I love you," it is most definitely taken as a form of romantic love, unless, for example, it is said by a parent to a child or vice versa or between friends. In many situations, it is not necessarily proper for a male friend to say to a female friend, "I love you," unless it is meant romantically. So how does one convey the love that you feel for a person when it is not romantic?

The Greek language goes beyond the English language and has four words that describe different types of love. These are *agape*, *philia*, *storge,* and *eros*. Agape is defined as a selfless, sacrificial, unconditional love, which is the highest of the four types of love. Eros is sensual love. Philia is a close friendship or brotherly love. Storge is family love. We could certainly benefit from having different words in the English language translating more accurately what we mean when we say or write the word *love*. However, when we add an adjective in front of love—like romantic, unconditional, or sisterly—it certainly goes a long way to define what we mean.

Let's take romantic love. This is a type of love that typically comes with conditions and wants and desires of the ego. For example, I love that person until she/he cheats on me, I love that man if he makes me laugh, I love that man if he is over six feet tall, or I love that woman if she has sex with me. Romantic love leads to sexual relationships that are characteristically based on our primal emotions and societal pressures to procreate.

Then there is the love of things, which usually describes an attachment that disappears when, for instance, the thing loses its shine or goes out of style. For example, I love the car until it breaks down, or I love those shoes until the next fashion trend. The love of things is typically based on what the ego wants, and the term *love*, in this context, is a strong emotion for an inanimate object.

The meaning of *love* and *I love you* can also vary from person to person. The meaning depends on how you grew up and your experiences throughout your life. One person may feel that saying "I love you" comes with terms, conditions, and expectations, such as "I love you if you love me" or "I love you but don't get too close."

Authentic Love is different from all examples described in the above three paragraphs. When a person says, "I love you," for no other reason than you are a human being and because of that you are worthy of love, that is Authentic Love. Authentic Love is the love that exists when there are no attachments or desires; it comes from the core of your being or soul where attachments and desires do not exist. Some may define this as unconditional love or a mother's love, but these two terms do not do Authentic Love justice. It is not just for parents and their love of a child, nor is it only unconditional. Anita Moorjani, in her book *Dying to Be Me*, explains that during her near-death experience she felt wrapped with love. She explained that the overuse of the term *unconditional love* has resulted in the phrase losing its intensity and that the "feeling of pure, unconditional *love* was unlike anything I'd known before" (Moorjani, 2012). She further went on to state that the love was undiscriminating, unqualified, and nonjudgmental. Therefore, she didn't have to prove herself to receive it or do anything to deserve it (Moorjani, 2012). This is Authentic Love.

Authentic Love is unconditional, nonsexual, nongrasping, accepting, selfless, endless, powerful, and so much more. It is the feeling we have when our egos are quiet, and thus it is not based on emotional desires. It is a feeling that we can have for our children, our partners, our parents, and strangers all around the world. It is also a state of being that one feels inter-mittently or consistently throughout one's life, or in the case of highly realized enlightened masters, it is felt constantly. Spiritual masters have alluded to the fact that this feeling, Authentic Love, can exist after death, as experienced by Anita Moorjani as described above. Authentic Love is the actual essence of who we are and why we are spiritual beings going through a human experience.

Many traditions provide insights as to what Authentic Love is. For example, in the Christian faith, the New International Version (NIV) of the Bible states, "[4]Love is patient, love is kind. It does not envy, it does not boast, it is not proud. [5]It does not dishonour others, it is not self-seeking, it is not easily angered, it keeps no records of wrongs. [6]Love does not delight in evil but rejoices with the truth. [7]It always protects, always trusts, always hopes, and always perseveres.[8] Love never fails" (1 Corinthians 13).

One of the main teachings of Tibetan Buddhism is the Four Immeasurables, or four divine states. Loving-kindness is one of these four, with compassion, joy, and equanimity being the other three. These four states represent the extraordinary states of the mind and are to be directed toward an immeasur-able amount of sentient beings. Practicing them will result in immense karma.

Authentic Love has the qualities of all four divine states. Compassion is the closest to Authentic Love, as further discussed in Chapter 2. In addition, Authentic Love does not discriminate. It is equal in its deliverance. Furthermore, joy is defined as the attitude that rejoices in the happiness of others, which is an element of Authentic Love. It is opposite of jeal-ousy and selfishness. Loving-kindness is the intent and wish to want the best for all beings—that they be happy and have good health, success, and friends and be free from suffering.

Therefore, Authentic Love has the qualities of all Four Immeasurables.

Thubten Chodron, a Buddhist nun and author of *Don't Believe Everything You Think: Living with Wisdom and Compassion,* states that the love that is generated on the Dharma path is unconditional. We simply want others to be happy without any strings attached, without expecting happiness in return or without any expectations that they do something for us in return (Thubten Chodron, 2012).

In addition, Nyanaponika Thera, a twentieth-century Theravadan Buddhist monk, in *The Four Sublime States: Contemplations on Love, Compassion, Sympathetic Joy and Equanimity,* provides further defining qualities of love or Authentic Love by stating:

Love, without desire to possess, knowing well that in the ultimate sense there is no possession and no possessor: this is the highest *love.*

Rather, *love* that lies like a soft but firm hand on the ailing beings, ever unchanged in its sympathy, without wavering, unconcerned with any response it meets. *Love* that is comforting coolness to those who burn with the fire of suffering and passion; that is life-giving warmth to those abandoned in the cold desert of loneliness, to those who are shivering in the frost of a loveless world; to those whose hearts have become as if empty and dry by the repeated calls for help, by deepest despair.

Love, that *is* strength and *gives* strength: this is the highest *love.*

Love, which by the Enlightened One was named "the liberation of the heart," "the most sublime beauty": this is the highest *love* (Nyanaponika Thera, 2013).

Baha'u'llah, founder of the Baha'i Faith, maintained that God's love is his own essence and that his love gives material existence, divine grace, and eternal life to all. Therefore, if love is part of God's essence and this love is the cause of eternal life and divinity for humans and animals, then this love is simply the reason for our existence in this life and after (Smith, 1999).

Adub'l-Baha, son of Baha'u'llah, also stated that love is the spiritual fulfillment, love is the light of the kingdom, and love is the cause of the manifestation of the truth. Furthermore, Adub'l-Baha wrote that love is the greatest power in the world of existence and the true source of external happiness (Smith, 1999). This love, as described by Baha'u'llah and Adub'l-Baha, can therefore be equated to what is described as Authentic Love.

In Islamic Sufism, unconditional love is the basis for the divine love (or Ishq-e-Haqeeqi), which means to love God unconditionally and selflessly. It also means to devote one's life to God and ask for nothing in return. Sufism and other religious traditions, therefore, describe a kind of divine love that parallels Authentic Love defined herein.

Qualities of Authentic Love

Authentic Love can be described and understood through its qualities. Authentic Love is not just a concept or a feeling; it is a state of being that one can grow into or realize when it is understood. These qualities are concepts and need to be realized, grasped, and applied collectively in order to comprehend Authentic Love. None of these qualities in isolation define what Authentic Love is.

The qualities of Authentic Love are described as:
1. selfless
2. unconditional
3. authentic, genuine and true
4. endless, infinite and timeless

5. the core of and imperative to our existence
6. our spiritual nature
7. a realization
8. an energy
9. not an emotion
10. generated by the soul, not the ego
11. accessible to and by everyone
12. voluntary and involuntary
13. the most power energy in the world
14. the Law of Attraction
15. not able to exist with anger or fear
16. healing
17. not romantic love, necessarily
18. not having an opposite
19. similar to compassion
20. not found in things
21. only exists in the present moment
22. a gift
23. reciprocity is automatic
24. non-discriminating
25. the source is you

1. Authentic Love Is Selfless

Authentic Love is selfless and altruistic. When one expresses Authentic Love, the intent is not that the self benefits but that the recipient does. It is felt and expressed with no regard for self but only for the well-being of the other. You may even have more Authentic Love for another person than you have for yourself. Authentic Love means giving without the thought or need for any gain. In Hinduism, it is believed that one gives up selfishness in love, not expecting anything in return. You want and seek the best for others and the betterment and benefit of all humans and other sentient beings.

2. Authentic Love Is Unconditional

Authentic Love is unconditional; there are no conditions or terms related to feeling Authentic Love for another. You demonstrate Authentic Love regardless of whether others love you back, treat you with respect, or act in a certain way. It does not matter whom the recipient of your Authentic Love is or if she or he reciprocates with Authentic Love for you. A mother's love for her child or the love exhibited by a dog to its owner are examples of the unconditional aspects of Authentic Love.

Being unconditional has characteristics related to also being nonjudgmental. When you are not judging, you see past the shortcomings and negative acts of the person you are feeling Authentic Love toward and only see their soul. Relatedly, by not judging a person, the unconditional nature of Authentic Love is more easily felt. There is no judgment in Authentic Love.

Authentic Love does not exist when there is attachment, because attachment is considered to be a condition. One cannot feel, give, or receive Authentic Love if there is a condition. When you have attachment to a person or attachment to the outcome of the Authentic Love given, Authentic Love cannot exist. Authentic Love facilitates freedom, not neediness for connection. Authentic Love can also be given to total strangers where there is no attachment.

3. Authentic Love Is Authentic, Genuine, and True

Authentic means undisputed origin, not false but genuine. Authentic Love is the origin or basis of who we are and what we need to survive as human beings. Everyone can feel it, and when it is felt, it is automatically known to be true. When you have Authentic Love and can recognize it, there is no question that it is Authentic Love. Furthermore, Authentic Love comes from the soul and, therefore, is natural and genuine.

Authentic Love is the only true reality. Some have expressed that it is the only true experience, which comes forth from the soul. When experienced, it feels right and correct. It feels indisputable.

Marianne Williamson, in *A Return to Love*, states that love is real and everything else is an illusion (Williamson, 1996). There is the belief that our spiritual existence is real and our physical existence is an illusion. What might sound counterintuitive could in fact be the truth. After all, when we die, there is a part of us that carries on (i.e., our spirit) while our bodies do not. Buddhists believe that in the physical existence, we live in an illusion, and we will continue to live in an illusion until we wake up. When we wake up and reach enlightenment, we will then understand the truth of our existence. There is also the belief that the truth of our existence is that we are Authentic Love and that in this human existence we are on a path to realize Authentic Love. To support this belief, Deepak Chopra, in *The Path to Love*, writes that our existence is an expression of love and that it is the only real expression our existence can have. "Everything else is an illusion" (Chopra, 1998).

4. Authentic Love Is Endless, Infinite, and Timeless

Authentic Love is endless and infinite. There is no set amount in the world or in an individual. It does not begin, and it does not end. It is.

Authentic Love exists regardless of space and time. It is all encompassing, not dependent on or determined by time, and therefore, it is timeless.

5. Authentic Love Is the Core of, and Imperative to, Our Existence

Authentic Love is what exists as our primary nature or state. The ultimate meaning of why we feel Authentic Love is beyond the knowledge of our current existence, yet it is essential to our existence. It makes us feel happy, peaceful, and content and gives meaning to our lives. Not only is Authentic Love the core of our existence, it is also the core of the universe. Anita Moorjani, in *Dying to Be Me*, states that in her near-death experience, she realized that "the entire universe is composed of unconditional love," that she is an expression of this unconditional love and that the universal life-force energy is love. She further states, "Every atom, molecule, quark, and teraquark, is made up of love" (Moorjani, 2012). She further surmises that because of this, she is also made of unconditional love.

Authentic Love is imperative to our very existence. We cannot survive without it. It has unfortunately been proven that when young primates and humans are not given Authentic Love, they do not survive. It is also proven that when we do not feel or receive Authentic Love, our existence is diminished and is fraught with emotional difficulties.

> Love and compassion are necessities, not luxuries. Without them, humanity cannot survive.
>
> — His Holiness the XIV Dalai Lama

6. Authentic Love Is Our Spiritual Nature

When we are not in this human existence, our consciousness exists with the Divine[1], where we are all inseparably linked. When we are born, we experience a form of separation from the Divine. The separation caused by birth is drastic and difficult. We then spend the rest of our lives seeking connections with lovers, parents, friends, community, work, or pets ... anything that helps us to not feel disconnected. Similarly, we seek someone to make us feel whole because we feel like something, or this connection, is missing. We also typically seek something, such as material wealth and success, to fill the void. What actually fills the void, what makes this connection, and what we are ultimately looking for is Authentic Love.

Authentic Love is the connection. Authentic Love is what we are and makes us one with the Divine and others. Authentic Love is our spiritual nature. It is

> Love is Spirit. Spirit is Self.
> —*The Path to Love* by
> Deepak Chopra

what we all strive to have and ultimately to be. The aspiration for the manifestation of the best in human nature is Authentic Love. As spiritual teachings convey, your spirit is pure love, Authentic Love. You need to identify with your spiritual nature in order to recognize that you are Authentic Love. That is the spiritual goal of life. Deepak Chopra, in *The Path to Love*, supports this by stating that the reason we do not totally feel loved or lovable is because we do not identify with our spiritual nature, which is love or Authentic Love (Chopra, 1998).

If Authentic Love is our spiritual nature, then why don't we just have it? We are all born with the capacity and ability to feel Authentic Love. However, the human body and mind have developed limitations to generating and receiving Authentic

Love. These limitations include allowing experiences to block our true nature.

Many psychologists and spiritual masters know that most of the issues that we experience in adulthood are based on something that happened to us in the past, in particular what happened to us in childhood. As an example, you feel unworthy or lack confidence in adulthood because your parents neglected you or because your parents or teachers told you that you wouldn't amount to anything. All of these past events that cause you issues now and in the future are the result of a lack of Authentic Love in childhood. When you are loved as a child and encouraged to love, confidence, worthiness, and emotional stability are the result.

No one has ever complained about problems caused by being truly loved. Have problems actually developed because someone showed us they cared, someone was understanding, or someone told us that we were worthy? All of these positive actions are signs and examples of Authentic Love. No one has ever truly felt that they feel hate or are confused because they received Authentic Love from their mother, grandfather, or partner.

Your true spiritual nature can be concealed by negativity. Where there is negativity, there is fear. Ultimately, all negativity and harmful emotions are a result of fear: fear of not being in control, fear of not being loved, fear of being hurt, and so on. These experiences are inevitable in this human existence. I don't know a single person who has not experienced fear and some kind of heartache. When this happens, your ego, because of the hurt that it feels, protects your heart by closing it. How you deal with these experiences will either open your spiritual nature and your ability to feel Authentic Love or close you to who you really are. You now have to learn how to open your heart again to feel Authentic Love.

Your capacity for Authentic Love might be covered up by the belief that you are not lovable and/or you cannot love. Belief and acceptance of your true nature as Authentic Love will

> Your tasks is not to seek for love, but merely to seek and find all the barriers within yourself that you have built against it.
>
> —Rumi

assist in the path to feel Authentic Love. Your life experiences, environment, and imposed and accepted belief system have covered up or hidden your Authentic Love. As a result, you have lost sight of your essence.

When you live entirely from Authentic Love, which many spiritual masters do, you are at one with the Divine and operate from the ultimate spiritual realization. When you are not operating from Authentic Love, this division is the source of all problems. This division, of not acting and reacting from Authentic Love, causes all of the negative emotions, such as fear, anger, jealousy, pride, spite, and so on, which are the causes of our difficulties.

There is the belief that we have come to this earth as souls in search of Authentic Love. Using a metaphor from the Christian tradition, they believe that we, as humans, fell from grace in the Garden of Eden as a result of our desires. This resulted in our egos taking over. The purpose of our earthly existence is to find Authentic Love or more aptly, go back to Authentic Love.

7. Authentic Love Is a Realization

Authentic Love is not a place or an evolution; it is a realization. You have it. You just might not know it. You are the source of Authentic Love. In some people, the realization unfolds gradually. In others, it can be more immediate and can occur due to specific circumstances, such as a major life event that causes the heart to crack open. Examples of major life events that can result in the realization of Authentic Love are the birth of one's child, illness diagnosis, or the death of a loved one.

Letting go of your resistance to feeling Authentic Love will result in feeling Authentic Love. Once you understand and accept that Authentic Love is your spiri-

> Love is always with you.
> —Thich Nhat Hanh

tual nature and that we all have it, it will manifest. The path to Authentic Love is everywhere. Everywhere is Authentic Love. You only need to realize this to discover that you already have Authentic Love.

8. Authentic Love Is Energy

Energy is something that is neither material nor physical. We cannot physically feel it with our five senses. We cannot see, touch, smell, hear or taste it. Authentic Love is also not material or physical. Identical to energy, Authentic Love cannot be known through our physical senses. Authentic Love can be demonstrated physically but can only be felt and expressed intuitively. We need to identify with it through our spiritual or intuitive sense. We can then understand when we feel it and when we don't.

Energy cannot be created or destroyed, but it can be transferred to the same or different forms. Like energy, Authentic Love cannot be created or destroyed. It just is. Authentic Love, as with energy, can travel from one being to another. You can feel Authentic Love inside, and you can receive it, as an energy force. You can intellectually know that you are being loved, but only you can feel it on the inside, intuitively.

Energy is also known as the strength and vitality required

for sustained mental or physical activity. Likewise, Authentic Love is the energy that allows us to survive and thrive emotionally. Furthermore, Authentic Love, like energy, cannot be grasped or held. You cannot physically possess Authentic Love. Also similar to energy, Authentic Love is fluid. Authentic Love is not fixed or static; it comes, goes, and flows.

The source of Authentic Love is the Divine. It is therefore transcendental, beyond the self. By tapping into Authentic Love, we find the inexhaustible source of life. Gary Zukav, in *The Seat of the Soul*, states that when one asks for love, it is same as asking for the soul's energy (Zukav, 2007).

All feelings and emotions are energy and therefore exist as a vibration. Harmful emotions, such as hate, anger, revenge, attachment, and jealousy, have a very low and negative vibration, which is not good for the body or the rest of the world. Authentic Love and positive emotions, such as compassion, peace, and joy, have a high vibrational energy. In fact, Authentic Love is the highest vibration, even greater than any of the positive emotions. As a result, Authentic Love is felt beyond these positive emotions.

9. Authentic Love Is Not an Emotion

All emotions are generated by the ego, and the ego is what we have acquired or developed for this human existence. The ego is not who we are. We are the one that is able to "see" the ego by how we act and react. If we can see how we act and react, then who is doing the watching? The soul is the watcher. The soul is who we are. In order for the ego to act and react, the ego does this based on the emotions that the ego feels. If we feel happy, fear, jealousy, rage, compassion, etc., our ego acts accordingly. The soul is, therefore, not actually generating the emotions, the ego is.

What the soul feels and is, is Authentic Love. Since the soul is Authentic Love, Authentic Love is not generated by the ego, and therefore, Authentic Love is not an emotion which can only be generated by the ego. Authentic Love, is the essence of who we are. For clarification, emotions are energy, as Authentic Love is energy. However, not all energies are emotions.

10. Authentic Love, the Ego, and the Soul

Authentic Love is generated by the soul. The soul is that part of you that exists when there is no ego or that is behind the ego, watching. It is that part of you that goes on after you die. It is that part of you that is Authentic Love.

Your ego is what feels emotions, both negative and positive. Feelings of anger, compassion, hate, jealousy, desire, and happiness are all felt from and created by the ego. Your ego, by primarily feeling through the five senses, is trying to make itself concrete. It is only interested in making itself real; this is the nature of the ego. For the ego to be real, it requires its needs to be met. By this very description, the ego is very selfish and self-centered. The ego, therefore, is not capable of generating Authentic Love. Authentic Love or the soul does not ask, "What is in it for me?" but the ego does.

Gary Zukav, in his book *The Seat of the Soul*, supports this notion by writing that the personality or ego can produce positive emotions in relation to others, but love, compassion, and wisdom are experiences of the soul, not the personality. This can be interpreted as Authentic Love, as experiences of the soul, since these three characteristics are components of Authentic Love. He further states that the soul's natural state is "compassion, clarity and boundless love" (Zukav, 2007).

Unbeknownst to the ego, it is constantly reaching for

Authentic Love. Since the ego does not know what it is seeking, it can then look in places and for things that result in pain, fear, addictions, and other psychological problems. More specifically, the ego unconsciously looks for Authentic Love where it thinks it exists: romance, sex, food, shopping, alcohol, and so on.

You do not need to consciously live from your soul to feel Authentic Love. You can still feel Authentic Love without knowing you are living from your soul, as there are many who feel Authentic Love but do not know what it is or can describe it as such. But consciously living from your soul, even if only for moments at a time, will increase your ability to feel, generate, and live with Authentic Love. The soul is Authentic Love, and removing the barriers that the ego erects is our path to Authentic Love.

11. Authentic Love Is Accessible to Everyone

There is not a human being on earth who has less access to Authentic Love or has less Authentic Love than anyone else. Everyone has equal access to Authentic Love, as we all have a soul. It may appear to be less accessible to some, but that's because their ego is doing a great job of covering it up. Authentic Love is only less obvious in those that are not living from their soul.

In modern Western society, we are taught that love and therefore, by connotation, Authentic Love is hard to find and that there may only be one chance at love. We are further taught that if we find it, we are lucky. Even in

> There is love enough in this world for everybody, if people will just look.
>
> — *Cat's Cradle* by Kurt Vonnegut

the context of romantic love, this notion is based on fear of not "finding" it. However, we all have Authentic Love. Not only is Authentic Love accessible to all, Authentic Love is the same in all of us. It is the same feeling and has the same results. It is the one, and the most important, commonality humans share. It is what ultimately defines as being "one" and connected.

12. Authentic Love Is Voluntary and Involuntary

Authentic Love is involuntary as perceived from the conscious mind. Sometimes the heart and soul simply feel Authentic Love. It just happens. New parents have said that they experienced it for their newborn child, newlyweds during their wedding vows, others when seeing a suffering child on television or during meditation. We don't know why we have Authentic Love for that specific person or generate it during those specific situations, but we do.

Authentic Love is also voluntary. In order to generate it consciously, we need to choose to feel Authentic Love. When we make this choice, we connect with our souls and with the Divine. By connecting with our souls, we have Authentic Love. When we consciously acknowledge that our spiritual goal is to feel Authentic Love, then we are on the path to Authentic Love. We also need to consciously remove the barriers our ego has built, and choosing to feel Authentic Love helps us remove these barriers. We can also voluntarily choose to feel Authentic Love for those whom we might not otherwise want to. This does not necessarily mean that it will happen easily, but the choice is one of the ingredients required for Authentic Love to occur.

This choice also allows for a mental connection between

> And whether we love, or close our hearts to love, is a mental choice we make, every moment of every day.
>
> — *A Return to Love* by Marianne Williamson

the mind and soul. If the heart, where the soul metaphorically resides, and mind are not in sync, Authentic Love will not occur. That is why we need conscious choice to feel Authentic Love.

13. The Most Powerful Energy in the World

Authentic Love is the most powerful energy in the world. It is even more powerful than hate, indifference, or any of the negative or positive emotions. Charles Hummel, in Rhonda Byrne's *The Secret*, states, "Thought impregnated with love is invincible" (Byrne, 2006). Gary Zukav, in *The Seat of the Soul,* states that love is the highest frequency and energy current (Zukav, 2007).

Authentic Love has been documented and demonstrated throughout history and can be exemplified in the following true stories:

- People have been able to conjure enormous physical strength to save someone they love.

> Love is the strongest force the world possesses and yet it is humblest imaginable.
>
> — Mahatma Gandhi

- A person saves a dog from a burning building.
- A twelve-year-old girl shaves her head so that her friend who lost her hair due to chemotherapy won't be embarrassed at school.
- A girl gave one of her kidneys to her father.
- A man sacrifices his life for the life of others.
- A woman gives her last morsel of food to her child during a famine.
- Doctors, nurses, and other people risk their lives to help others through an epidemic.

• People help whales that are stuck in a small, open patch of ice.

No other story, whether expe-rienced or just heard, moves us like Authentic Love stories. Nega-tive stories may move us, but they are steeped in emotions such as anger, bewilderment, and hate, where Authentic Love cannot reside. No emotion can compete with the power of Authentic Love. Once Authentic Love is felt, you believe you can do and be anything. One of the benefits of Authentic Love is the increased inner strength and clarity that helps you to not get bogged down by fear or hate or jealousy. Now that is power.

> Where ther is great love, there are always miracles.
>
> — *Death Comes for the Archbishop* by Willa Cather

Authentic Love is the highest frequency, and therefore you are harnessing the greatest power in existence. Love, spirit, and power are one; it doesn't get much stronger or better than that. Great spiritual masters, such as Buddha, Jesus, and Krishna, knew the power of Authentic Love. They were all messengers of Authentic Love, and having Authentic Love allowed them to do what they did and become who they became.

14. The Law of Attraction

Rhonda Byrne, author of *The Secret*, says that the law of attrac-tion is also known as the law of love. If you think thoughts of love, love will come to you, through yourself and from others (Byrne, 2006). The premise of *The Secret* is that whatever you think and feel, you attract. If you think and feel jealousy, you will think and feel more jealousy, and jealousy will come to you. Then, if you think and feel Authentic Love, you will think and feel more Authentic Love, and more Authentic Love will come to you.

Gary Zukav supports this theory in *The Seat of the Soul* by stating that everyone draws to them personalities with consciousness of similar frequencies. He also calls this the law of attraction where like attracts like. Therefore, an angry person has a life filled with angry people, and a loving person has a life filled with loving people (Zukav, 2007).

> Amor gignit amorem.
> (Love begets love.)
>
> — Unknown

15. Authentic Love Cannot Exist with Anger or Fear

Authentic Love cannot exist in a heart that has anything negative in it, such as anger, bitterness, impatience, or fear. Since the heart can only feel one emotion at a time, the negative emotion in your heart puts up a barrier to any other feeling. You cannot feel compassion and anger at once. You can, however, go from one emotion to another in a split second.

Try sitting down and think about anger. Think of a time when you were angry. For example, anger can flare up for me when I'm driving. If I get cut off, if the slower traffic does not stay in the right lane, or if traffic keeps me from getting where I

> There is no fear in love; but perfect love casteth out fear.
>
> —1 John 4:18, NIV

want to go, I feel anger. See how your body feels when it is angry. Is your heart rate affected? How does your chest or your head feel? Does it put you in a bad state for the rest of the day? How easy is it for you to switch from anger to a positive emotion, such a joy?

Now try sitting with love (don't worry if it is Authentic Love or not). Think of someone you love, a child, a spouse, your mother, or a pet. Can you feel it in your heart or mind? Does it make you feel stressed or joyful? I think of my son, and my heart expands and feels warm. It feels like my heart is radiating

> Love is the total absence of fear.
>
> — *Love Is Letting Go of Fear* by Gerald Jampolsky

from my chest. I feel calm, peaceful, content, and at ease. There is no negative emotion when I am in that space of love.

There is the belief that the feeling of separateness from others generates fear. Throughout our lives, we are inundated with the notion that we are all separate entities, not connected human beings. This feeling of separateness results in a fear of others and makes it extremely difficult for us to generate Authentic Love for others or feel that Authentic Love is directed toward us. When fear of separation (or separation) occurs, a sense of sadness or depression can set in. As human beings, we are wired for connection to survive and thrive, and when we believe we are separate, it affects our sense of well-being. With Authentic Love, we do not feel separate, as there is a definite connector, and we have no fear. Fear cannot exist in the light of Authentic Love.

16. Healing Power of Authentic Love

Authentic Love, as the energy of the soul, can heal anything that results from negative emotions, including actually healing the ego causing the negative emotions. There is nothing that cannot be healed by Authentic Love. Authentic Love brings more than peace. It removes all the issues of the ego, leaving only the best behind, such as concern for others, contentment, compassion, and forgiveness. When one feels Authentic Love, there is no space for harmful emotions. Therefore, the more we have Authentic Love, the less we will have adverse feelings.

Violence, hatred, and ultimately fear can be healed only by
Authentic Love. There are many
examples of humans trying to
end violence through more

> Love and compassion are the
> pillars of world peace.
>
> — *His Holiness, the*
> *XIV Dalai Lama*

violence and by exerting greater strength with no success. Yet
all of the world's problems are a result of negative emotions,
which are nothing other than a lack of Authentic Love. The
world's problems come from the emotions of each and specific
human beings. The world itself does not feel negativity.
Therefore, resolving the issues in the hearts of individuals can
solve the world's problems.

From an individual perspective, think of an emotion that
has caused a difficulty—for example, jealousy, anger, righteousness, and competition. When experiencing a state of jealousy, either you or the person that is jealous of you cannot feel
Authentic Love. When in anger, clearly there is no Authentic
Love. With righteousness, one person makes an assumption of
being right, and therefore the other person is wrong. No
Authentic Love there either. When one feels a sense of competition, there is no Authentic Love because one person wants to
defeat and be better than the other. Therefore, all the world's
atrocities and conflicts are caused by a lack of Authentic Love,
nothing else.

Children who do not experience Authentic Love grow up
with difficulty in adjusting to their exterior and interior
worlds. They have not been taught, shown, or felt Authentic
Love through example. They do not know how to generate
Authentic Love within themselves, for themselves, and for
others. These children need to learn, talk about, and experience Authentic Love. They need to know what it is and what is
missing inside of them. They need to know how to generate it
-- that is how they will heal.

For adults to heal, we need to be conscious of our feelings and understand what triggers our negative emotions and why. Like children, we need to know how to generate Authentic Love. Chapter 7 shows how this can be done.

Deepak Chopra, in *The Path to Love*, writes that with respect to love, scientific evidence demonstrates that love is as potent as medicine and that the results are dramatic when love is present and when it is withdrawn

> Love is the biggest eraser I know. Love erases even the deepest and most painful memories because love goes deeper than anything else.
>
> — *The Power Is Within You* by Louise Hay

(Chopra, 1998). He further writes that feelings of love aid in recovery. Studies in cardiac units have shown that when male patients respond positively when asked if they feel love, they are more likely to recover than those who responded negatively (Chopra, 1998). In addition, he states that having a pet to love reduces illness and depression of those living in retirement homes, and older people feel that when they have something to love, they have a greater purpose in life (Chopra, 1998).

Authentic Love is needed to heal individuals, emotionally and physically. Gary Zukav, in *The Seat of the Soul*, states that we will eventually understand that love heals everything and all there is, is love (Zukav, 2007). With the healing of each individual, a shift will occur. The shift will affect all of those who are in contact with Authentic Love. Each shift will change the world for the better.

You may say the world is getting more violent, but in actual fact it is not. There has been a significant decline in war-related deaths over the last two centuries. In 1946, there were forty-six democratic countries, which has now risen to over one hundred (Pinker, 2011). In addition, our IQs are getting higher with each generation, leading to the decrease in violence (Pinker, 2011). Furthermore, the change in communications and media over the last fifty years has resulted in us being inundated with news—bad news, when actually there is much more good going on in the world than bad. Good news is just not reported over our standard means of communication. In addition, over the last fifty years, more laws have been passed, more books have been published, more discussions have taken place on tolerance, equality, religious freedom, and yes, even love. Gina Lake, in *Radiance,* writes, "Humanity is evolving, and it is evolving toward love" (Lake, 2006). We are progressing as individuals and communities on the path of Authentic Love, benefitting and healing ourselves and others.

17. Romantic Love Is Not Authentic Love, Necessarily

Authentic Love is not the same as romantic love. Authentic Love can exist in a romantic relationship as long as the other characteristics that make up Authentic Love are present. Furthermore, whereas sex is part of a romantic relation, Authentic Love has no relationship to sex.

> We waste time looking for the perfect lover, instead of creating the perfect love.
>
> — *Still Life with Woodpecker* by Tom Robins

We first need to ask why the first stage of romantic love is what we imagine we want, or desire, to have. It makes us feel so good, so special, and our hearts soar or ache with happiness. Falling in love provides greater insight into who you really are because this experience can be the closest thing to Authentic Love that many of us may feel -- that is why we long for it and mourn it so deeply when we lose it.

The experience of falling in love and its associated emotions are why so many people are obsessed with romantic love and sex. The first rush of romantic love can make people believe they are experiencing Authentic Love. But until Authentic Love is understood for what it actually is, people will continue to look for Authentic Love in romance and sex. Romantic love and sex are the two things that bring us closer together physically but not necessarily spiritually.

Sometimes we believe that romantic love is selfless. But as many of us have realized, romantic love is not selfless; it is actually selfish. Romantic love wants to be reciprocated. Romantic love is based on conditions, including the way the other person looks and acts. Therefore, romantic love is not often and not necessarily Authentic Love.

However, romantic love can point to or provide a glimpse into Authentic Love. Romantic love can also give us a taste of Authentic Love, during the early stages when people typically feel selfless and altruistic, and their love can be unconditional. If those qualities are sustained, Authentic Love is possible with two people who are in a romantic relationship.

Falling in love can be a spiritual experience. The Divine nature of falling in love, which is prevalent in other cultures and documented throughout history, appears to be lost in our Western culture. In order to fall in love and similarly to feel Authentic Love, an opening in the heart needs to occur. This opening reveals, or allows us to live from, the soul. When we look for love, we are actually looking for a spiritual realization. Falling in love and experiencing Authentic Love is about seeing the spirit, or the Divine nature, in someone else and also seeing it in yourself and wanting someone to see your Divine nature in you.

There is the belief that romantic love coupled with Authentic Love is an elusive phenomenon. However, this is not necessary true. If you want Authentic Love—truly want it

—it is there. It seems elusive because very few understand what it actually is, accessible and available to all.

In our Western society, finding a suitable partner, getting married, and raising a family is not necessarily a spiritual path but a societal norm. In most countries and cultures, getting married and having children is expected. Romantic love associated with the societal norm, when based on expectations, conditions, and requirements, is not Authentic Love. It is based on personal or societal needs. Unless the relationship is based on the principles of Authentic Love but also without expectations of fulfillment (i.e., making oneself whole), it is not Authentic Love. If the relationship has Authentic Love and is coupled with the intent to grow spiritually for oneself and the other, this is a true spiritual partnership.

18. There Is No Opposite to Authentic Love

Since Authentic Love is the essence of life, there can be no opposite. There cannot be an un-essence of life. All of the emotions do have an opposite, but Authentic Love is not an emotion. Neither fear, nor hate, nor anger is the opposite of Authentic Love. Courage is the opposite of fear, kindness is the opposite of hate, and joy is the opposite of anger. There is no opposite of Authentic Love.

19. Authentic Love and Compassion

Many confuse Authentic Love with compassion. According to the *Merriam-Webster Dictionary*, compassion is the "sympathetic consciousness of others' distress

> Love and compassion are pillars of world peace.
>
> — His Holiness, the XIV Dalai Lama

together with a desire to alleviate it." Based on this definition, there are several differences that separate Authentic Love from compassion. First, compassion is an emotion, and Authentic Love is not. Second, compassion can be conditional, as it is typically given to those that one feels is deserving, and Authentic Love is completely unconditional. Third, compassion can be based on attachment to, for example, a family member or close friend only. Authentic Love, by its nature, is based on nonattachment. Fourth, Authentic Love for someone does not include the desire to alleviate his or her suffering as Authentic Love does not have desires and is not discriminating.

However, compassion is the closest emotion to Authentic Love. The feeling of compassion is a definite step toward feeling and understanding what Authentic Love is. When someone's feelings or story affects you and causes you to be compassionate toward them, it opens the heart and the path toward Authentic Love.

Furthermore, compassion is dualistic because it is based on a feeling for another emphasizing separateness. Compassion does not necessarily understand the oneness of all beings. When you have compassion and integrate it with an understanding of the connection or oneness of everything with nonattachment and without conditions, your compassion then turns to Authentic Love.

20. Authentic Love Is Not Found in Things

The aching need for Authentic Love and the lack of Authentic Love drives us to look for Authentic Love in many ways -- sex, drugs, alcohol, shoes, purses, cars, and so on. We have this notion that things will be able to fill a void. Once we have these things, they eventually lose their luster, we tire of them, or we realize the emptiness still exists. These material objects and physical needs do not fill the void because what everyone is looking for is Authentic Love. Only Authentic Love makes you feel full, content, and at peace and removes the feeling of a void.

This notion is supported by Marianne Williamson in *A Return to Love* where she writes that the experience of love is a choice, and when we make that choice, we strive to find or obtain things that will make us happy. We soon come to realize that the external searching and acquisitions do not make us happy. Only internal love is the source of our happiness (Williamson, 1996).

21. Authentic Love Only Exists in the Present Moment

Authentic Love only exits and can only be generated in the moment. Like any other type of energy, Authentic Love does not exist in the past or the future. The past and future do not actually exist, except as a memory and desire, respectively; therefore, Authentic Love exists only in the present moment. When causes and conditions exist in the moment to facilitate Authentic Love, Authentic Love is generated. Thus, it can be instantaneous and spontaneous.

Since Authentic Love is generated in a moment, it can also disappear in a moment. It takes one word, one memory, or one action to close your heart and stop the flow of Authentic Love. Also, since Authentic Love only exists in the present moment, it can't be accumulated, saved, or stored. If this were possible, you would be able to bring Authentic Love from the present by saving or storing it and carrying it into a moment in the future where it could then be used. Since this is not possible, the benefit is that Authentic Love is always available, as we are always in the present moment.

22. Authentic Love Is a Gift

Authentic Love is not an entitlement, nor can one demand it. The presence of Authentic Love benefits the one who generates it and receives it; therefore, it is a gift. Authentic Love is an actual true gift, as a true gift is one that is given without any expectations of what the recipient is going to do with the gift. It doesn't matter if the recipient is going to say thank you or understand the enormity of the gift. With no expectations or conditions, Authentic Love is a gift, and a gift is Authentic Love.

23. Reciprocity is Automatic

Authentic Love is only received when Authentic Love is realized in your heart and from your soul. Without knowing what Authentic

> I believe love expands. As you give love out, it's recieved and reciprocated - and it grows. That's the beauty of it. Love is an energy. You can feed it to people, and they in turn feed it to others and eventually it comes back.
>
> — Hill Harper

Love is, you won't be able to recognize it. If you are given money, but you only see paper, you won't be able to obtain the benefits of the money. Have you ever known someone who is loved deeply through Authentic Love but doesn't acknowledge it or give it back to that person giving the Authentic Love?

Similarly, you can't receive Authentic Love without giving it. If you have Authentic Love, then by its very nature, it is given. If you don't have Authentic Love, then the heart is closed and you do not have access to your soul. Since Authentic Love is received or intuited through your heart and felt through your soul, if your heart is closed and your soul is inaccessible, you cannot receive or give Authentic Love.

24. Authentic Love and Equanimity

Authentic Love does not pick and choose to whom it is going to send this feeling. Authentic Love does not believe that some are deserving and some are not. It is

> Love your neighbour as yourself.
>
> — Mark 12:31 NIV

unconditional, so it expresses this feeling to all, equally. Since we are all one and connected with the Divine, we will ultimately have Authentic Love for everyone, including ourselves.

By restricting who you feel Authentic Love for, you are limiting your spiritual growth and limiting the results of Authentic Love, including peace and contentment. In *Soul to Soul*, Gary Zukav supports this premise by writing that by restricting your love to certain people, for whatever reason, you are preventing yourself from experiencing your ability to love. Love cannot be experienced in moderation, as it is unlimited. This can be done by having an open heart (Zukav, 2008). Furthermore, Anita Moorjani, in her book *Dying to Be Me,* explains that during her near-death experience, the love she felt was undiscriminating, and she felt that she did not have to do anything or prove herself deserving of it (Moorjani, 2012).

Equanimity is one of the Four Immeasurables in Buddhism, and realizing these states of being results in spiritual growth. Essentially, equanimity means that you do not differentiate between friends, family,

> A new commandment I give you: Love one another. As I have loved you, you also are to love one another.
>
> — John 13:34 NIV

strangers, and enemies. All human beings, actually all sentient beings, are to be treated equally. Equanimity is imperative to experience Authentic Love, receive the benefits of Authentic Love, and grow to your highest spiritual potential.

25. Source of Authentic Love Is You

Both children and adults typically look to someone else to give them attention, affection, and Authentic Love. While this may fulfill the ego, eventually one will have a feeling of loss or hollowness when it is only expected from others. This emptiness is caused by not feeling Authentic Love. When Authentic Love is felt internally, the void is filled and a sense of contentment is felt. One cannot strive for Authentic Love externally, because it does not exist out there. Therefore, the source is none other than one's self, through one's soul. To further expand upon this, since our souls are connected to the Divine, Authentic Love comes from both our souls and the Divine, which in actuality is connected to every other soul.

Since we are one, connected to the Divine, Authentic Love does not come from outside of us. Most of us have this notion of self and other, or dualism. In truth, dualism does not exist, and therefore Authentic Love comes from the self, which is part of all others. Furthermore, separation calls upon Authentic Love to bridge the gap or fill in the hole in our hearts, which then enhances the spiritual connection between all of us.

In the End, Authentic Love Is All That Matters

In the end, Authentic Love is all that matters. In the end, when everything else slips away, what most matters is who you have around you and the Authentic Love that you have given. Upon death, many reflect on their lives, and what matters most to them is the Authentic Love they shared with others. Shouldn't this be all that matters in life as well? If given the opportunity to reflect before we all die, how important is Authentic Love to you?

Once you have linked yourself with love, a flood of inspiration is revealed to you, whatever the subject, whatever the problem in life may be. Whatever it be that your eye casts its glance upon, it will disclose itself. Then you are on the real road, and what a joy this is!
—Hazrat Inayat Khan

[1] Throughout this book, I have used the term *Divine* to mean the ultimate spiritual place or being or existence. Please feel free to change this term to whatever term you are comfortable with, such as *higher self*, *God*, *Buddha dharma*, *universal consciousness*, and so on.

2. WHAT IS SELF AUTHENTIC LOVE?

You yourself, as much as anybody in the entire universe, deserve your love and affection.
—Gautama Buddha

SELF AUTHENTIC LOVE is the same as Authentic Love, except it is directed toward yourself as opposed to others. Essentially, the same principles, definitions, and qualities as discussed in chapter 2 apply to self Authentic Love.

While this chapter may be one of the smaller chapters in this book, don't think it is one of the least important chapters. In fact, this is one of the most important chapters because if you don't have Authentic Love for yourself, you are restricted from having Authentic Love for others. The self Authentic Love you have for yourself is reflective of the Authentic Love you are capable of giving to others. If you have no Authentic Love for yourself, you cannot give Authentic Love to others. If you have a little Authentic Love for yourself, you can give a little Authentic Love to others. If you have complete Authentic Love for yourself, you can give complete Authentic Love to others.

One of the characteristics of Authentic Love is equanimity. Authentic Love is felt for everyone, including you. You are no different from anyone else. We are all deserving, and everyone is valued equally. Since we are all equal, we need to put ourselves and others first and have Authentic Love for ourselves and others equally.

Self Authentic Love allows one to reciprocate Authentic Love and to perceive people in need of kindness and in need of Authentic Love. These people are then able to give Authentic Love freely, without fear of being hurt, fear of being used, feeling selfish, or feeling egotistical. As Louise Hay states in *The Power Is within You*, "It is not selfish to love ourselves. It clears us so that we can love ourselves enough to love other people" (Hay, 1991).

Conditions for Self Authentic Love

As with Authentic Love for others, the same conditions to feel self Authentic Love apply as discussed above. However, several are highlighted here. Firstly, that inside chatter, which is your ego, that judges you for what you do or makes you feel inferior or ashamed needs to stop at least enough to allow for the realization of the presence of Authentic Love for oneself to occur. Eventually, the goal is to completely stop the negative chatter about oneself, but only a few moments at a time is all that is needed to start the process of self Authentic Love.

Secondly, as discussed in chapter 2, the frequency of negative emotions needs to be reduced in order to feel self Authentic Love. As with Authentic Love for others, self Authentic Love exists in the absence of the negative emotions (e.g., fear, anger, jealousy, judgment, etc.). Negative emotions are reduced by examining them to find out why they are occurring and understanding that they are generated by the ego, not the soul. Only you, and no one else, can manage your harmful emotions. This takes work, time, and attention.

If you feel jealousy or resentment for others who have and receive what is perceived as love, you do not have Authentic Love. When you understand that everyone is deserving, you will realize that you are deserving and you will feel Authentic Love for yourself and others. What you feel inside is what you will also receive from the outside.

Thirdly, don't misconstrue the idea that if you give everything to others with no thought of yourself that this is Authentic Love. Giving love to others while putting others first and acting like a martyr is not Authentic Love or self Authentic Love. The action of putting oneself last is associated with a feeling of unworthiness, guilt, and possibly even shame. It leaves one with a sense of powerlessness and in some, neediness, which is far from self Authentic Love.

Discomfort of Loving Oneself

Self Authentic Love is a difficult concept for many people to grasp, understand, or generate. For many also, loving oneself can feel very uncomfortable. Typically, this is due to guilt, self-doubt, and feelings of unimportance. If you are finding that Authentic Love for yourself is difficult or it makes you feel some discomfort, an understanding of why you are feeling this way is essential. After, a release of that reason or those reasons that are holding you back from self Authentic Love is needed. Figuring out why you are feeling uncomfortable takes contemplation and honesty. During any process to a goal, I have always found it helpful if I have an affirmation of what I want to achieve. An example of an affirmation in this instance could be "sometime in the future, I will feel self Authentic Love" which should eventually be changed to "I feel self

Authentic Love". Affirmations, either by regularly stating them out loud or writing them out, provide the clear intent of what you want, which by the law of attraction will eventually occur.

Depending on the reason(s) you do not have Authentic Love for yourself, forgiveness may be necessary to release the reason(s) and to be successful in the healing process. If you grew up without Authentic Love from

> When you forgive and let go, not only does a huge weight drop off your shoulders, but the doorway to your own self-love opens.
>
> —*The Power Is Within You* by Louise Hays

your parents, there may not be the opportunity to discuss this with them, which otherwise may aid in forgiveness and healing. If you are like a friend of mine, Mark, the results of not having Authentic Love from your parents can cause emotional issues that creep up out of nowhere. One day, Mark felt angry toward his mother for no reason until he sat down to meditate to try to understand the source of the anger. He realized that his anger was related to the superficial hug he received that day from his mother, which in turn reminded him of the lack of love he felt as a child. He then realized three sequential insights: 1) he can never get that time back from his childhood to change his experiences to feel safe, secure, worthy, and loved; 2) he may never feel like he is receiving Authentic Love from his mother; and 3) the only thing that is possible and that will help is having self Authentic Love.

As stated by Louise Hay in *You Can Heal Your Life*, "When people come to me with a problem, I don't care what it is— poor health, lack of money, unfulfilling relationships or stifled creativity—there is only one thing I ever work on and that is LOVING THE SELF ... Love is the miracle cure. Loving ourselves works miracles in our lives" (Hay, 1999).

Furthermore, Anita Moorjani, in *Dying to Be Me*, states that in her near-death experience, she recognized that she is an expression of the unconditional love that makes up the entire universe. She further states that when we know we are love, having love for others and oneself is automatic. She further writes that love for oneself is not selfish or egotistical but in fact "[s]elfishness comes from lack of self-love" (Moorjani, 2012). If Authentic Love is who we are, our ego is being selfish by not letting us love ourselves.

For me, real self Authentic Love occurred when I felt I was devoid of Authentic Love from others. I was just about to turn fifty years old, and although I had done much self-reflection my whole life and even though I thought I had come to terms with the lack of Authentic Love in my childhood, it came back. I was having difficulties with my aging father and I even had a discrepancy with my spiritual teacher over an incident that I thought she would understand. This compounded with the fact that I did not have a partner at the time, resulted in making me feel less loved. All these factors, even though I knew I had the love of my thirteen-year-old son, left me feeling alone and totally unloved. Reaffirmation of self Authentic Love came when I realized that the Authentic Love had to come from me and that I was enough. It was extremely profound. This was further emphasized while reading Anita Moorjani's *Dying to be Me,* where she understood that you didn't have to do anything to deserve love and that love was always surrounding her (Moorjani, 2012). I recognized that I too am a beautiful being and just that fact that I existed made me worthy of love. This profound feeling came through me, not from outside of me.

Learn to love yourself – you won't regret it.

3. WHY DO WE NEED AUTHENTIC LOVE?

> This is a deep, permanent human condition,
> this need to be loved and to love.
> —Annie Proulx

AUTHENTIC LOVE IS necessary for two reasons: for physical/emotional survival and spiritual survival. Without Authentic Love, we can actually die and at the very least have a poor quality of life, both physically and emotionally. For spiritual survival, since we are spiritual beings and our souls are Authentic Love, we need to tap into Authentic Love to meet the purpose of our spiritual existence.

Two viewpoints, the scientific perspective and the spiritual perspective, support the need for Authentic Love. While no individual or ideology has actually used the term *Authentic Love* in its studies or perspectives, they are clearly talking about a love that is not just your standard affection with conditions, attachments, and selfish sentiments. They are clearly referring to what has been termed here as *Authentic Love*. Therefore, I have taken liberty in using this term in this chapter.

Science Perspective

During the first half of the twentieth century, many psychologists thought that showing love, affection, and attention to a child had no real purpose. It was felt that this was just a sentimental gesture. There was even the belief that physical contact with a child would only spread diseases and lead to psychological problems in adulthood.

Since the first half of the twentieth century, there have been numerous scientific studies on love, in particular what occurs when we are deprived of experiencing love. One of the preeminent studies was completed by John Bowlby in 1951, where he was commissioned by the World Health Organization to write a report on homeless children in Europe. The result of the report, which was published in the publication titled *Maternal Care and Mental Health*, was that infants or young children need to experience a warm, intimate, and continuous relationship with their mother (Bowlby, 1951).

In subsequent studies on cognitive science, development psychology, and evolutionary biology, Bowlby developed his attachment theory (Bowlby, 1958; Bowlby, 1959; Bowlby, 1960). This theory suggests that bonds formed early by children and their parents and caregivers have an immense impact on the child, which they then carry throughout their lives. Bowlby also postulated that the attachment of a mother to an infant and an infant to a mother actually improves the child's chances of survival. Furthermore, when the mother is responsive to the child's needs, the child feels a sense of security. It is this experience of dependability and security that allows the child to explore the world. Bowlby also suggests that the attachment facilitates other attachments the child will have later in life.

Bowlby's work also influenced the work of Mary

Ainsworth, who made major contributions to the attachment theory. In 1967, Ainsworth wrote *Infancy in Uganda: Infant Care and the Growth of Love,* which was one of the most significant studies in child psychiatry in the twentieth century (Ainsworth, 1967). This study showed that in the early years of a child's life, the quality of parental care is of great importance to the child's future mental health. If children are deprived of love and attention, their future mental health will be seriously threatened and they, subsequently, will pass that on to their children. Ainsworth correlates the plight of mental deprivation on children as similar in effect as would be felt by disease. Children need Authentic Love to become mentally stable adults, and if they do not receive Authentic Love, it is just as detrimental as experiencing an illness.

Ainsworth further goes on to state that as of 1967, no country has addressed this problem, even in so-called advanced countries. She states that there appears to be a tolerance for conditions of bad mental hygiene in hospitals, institutions, and nurseries, which if it was clearly known would result in public outcry (Ainsworth, 1967). We need to understand that serious social problems exist because many don't even know that Authentic Love exists, let alone understand the fact that Authentic Love is needed for social and mental stability.

Another notable example of what happens with a lack of Authentic Love occurred during the early part of the twentieth century at a hospital in Germany. During this time, numerous babies were brought into hospitals with unknown illnesses. Sadly, eventually these infants would waste away and pass. When Dr. Fritz Talbot of the Children's Clinic in Dusseldorf was confronted with these cases of children who were wasting away with no signs of success from traditional medicine, he would prescribe time with Old Anna. Old Anna was a matronly woman who would spend time cradling and hugging these children. She had more success in "curing" these children than the doctors or nurses had (Field, 1995).

In the 1960s, Harry Harlow, in the *Nature of Love*, demonstrated the powerful effects of love (Harlow, 1961). However, as a warning, by today's standards it would be considered animal cruelty. Harlow, by depriving young rhesus monkeys of contact with another being, showed extremely devastating effects. He revealed that the effects of deprivation lead to long-term profound psychological and emotional distress and even death. His experiments clearly revealed the importance of a mother's love for healthy childhood development.

The work and studies of Harlow, Bowlby, and Ainsworth helped influence key changes in how orphanages, adoption agencies, social services groups, and child care providers approached the care of children. While we have made some progress in the general acceptance that love, or actually Authentic Love, leads to more stable human beings and some of our institutions (e.g., orphanages) have made modifications to provide a more nurturing environment for children, we need to make more advances in these institutions and the foster care system. Caregivers and foster parents are not screened for their ability to provide Authentic Love, which is necessary for raising emotionally healthy children. In fact, our own homes may not be providing the necessary Authentic Love. How many parents discuss Authentic Love or the qualities of Authentic Love at the dinner table or when we have a heart-to-heart discussion with our children?

Additional and more recent studies further support the importance of Authentic Love in childhood development. In 2012, Joan Luby at the Washington University School in St. Louis, in her article titled *Maternal Support in Early Childhood Predicts Larger Hippocampal Volumes at School Age*, stated that nurturing children in early life may help them develop a large hippocampus (Luby, 2012). The hippocampus is a part of the brain, which is important for learning, memory, and stress responses.

Further studies have shown that children raised in a nurturing environment typically do better in school and are more emotionally developed than their non-nurtured peers. One of these studies was completed by Ronald Rohner, titled *Transnational Relations Between Perceived Parental Acceptance and Personality Dispositions of Children and Adults: A Meta-Analytic Review,* where he found that a father's love, or lack thereof, has a significant effect on the child's emotional development (Rohner, 2012). The child can actually be more aggressive, hostile, and insecure and have greater anxiety when there is a lack of love.

Other studies have shown that children who do not receive Authentic Love at a young age can still move on to productive, successful lives when loving, caring, and supportive relationships enter their lives (Bernard, 1995). In *A General Theory of Love* about the science of human emotions and biological psychiatry, Thomas Lewis, Fari Amini, and Richard Lannon document the importance and relativeness of love (Lewis, Amini, and Lannon, 2001). They determined that our brain chemistry and nervous system are measurably affected by those closest to us, and our systems synchronize with one another in a way that has profound implication for personality and lifelong emotional health.

In 1987, Hazan and Shaver published an article titled *Romantic Love Conceptualized as an Attachment Process* (Hazan and Shaver, 1987). They argued that the type of relationship the adult has in romantic relationships is similar to the type of relationship they had with their parents. The three major types of relationship attachments include secure, avoidant, and ambivalent. When a child experiences one of these types of attachments, the child is more likely to carry this one, or similar one, into his/her adult relationships. Hence, the proof that Authentic Love in infancy and early childhood is important for successful future relationships.

In a subsequent study by Fraley and Shaver in 2000, five issues related to the previous theory in Hazan and Shaver in 1987 provided further clarification on the nature and evolution of attachment relationships (Fraley and Shaver, 2000). Essentially, they found that when the caregiver is near, responsive, attentive, and loving, the child, and later the adult, feels secure, loving, and confident. The child then shows aspects of playfulness, less inhibition, happiness exhibited through smiling, sociability, and exploration. They further found that the cycle continues to the child's child. That is, the child-turned-adult is then near, responsive, attentive, and loving to his or her child.

When the caregiver is not near, responsive, attentive, or loving, the child feels anxiety and experiences separation distress. Subsequently, the child, and then the grown adult, inhibits emotional expression and attachment behaviors. These behaviors are then passed down to their children. This negative cycle needs to end and can end. Knowledge of what Authentic Love is, why we need it, and how to generate it will take us all out of this cycle.

Other studies have proven the benefits of Authentic Love. Studies conducted by Masaru Emoto show how feelings of love, or actually Authentic Love, can

> Love is a great beautifier.
>
> — *Little Women* by Louisa May Alcott

benefit the planet and us physically (Emoto, 2001). In the 1990s, the studies he conducted revealed that feelings of love can affect us physically. An experiment was completed where scientists talked to water and treated water according to how they spoke. One group treated the water kindly and spoke to the water with endearments such as "I love you" and "thank you." After a period of time, the water was analyzed, and it was found that the water crystals became clear and beautifully formed when the water was frozen. The other group spoke negatively to the water by saying such things as "I hate you" or "you idiot." When frozen, these water crystals formed dark, ugly holes. Since the human body is approximately 65 percent water, imagine the benefits when the water molecules are perfectly formed as opposed to malformed.

Paul J. Zak, in *The Moral Molecule: The Source of Love and Prosperity*, studied the chemistry of love (Zak, 2012). He found that oxytocin, which is released when love is felt, is responsible for actions such as trustworthiness, compassion, charity, and generosity. Oxytocin is also a motivator to think and do for others. In fact, your brain releases oxytocin when someone does something for you that then triggers you to do nice things for others, even if you do not know who initially did the thoughtful act. Zak's experiment actually shows that we have the capacity to love anyone and everyone.

Zak further found that those who release oxytocin are happier than those who release less oxytocin. Those with more oxytocin have better relationships and have been shown to be nicer to strangers. Furthermore, oxytocin is released when you are having a positive interaction with people, whether they are friends, family, or strangers. Oxytocin makes us care about others. It has been further shown to motive us to work together for a common purpose (Zak, 2012).

Love and negativity were also found to change our genetic code, DNA. Dr. Glen Rein, in the *Effect of Conscious Intention on Human DNA*, found that when one feels negative emotions, for example, stress, anxiety, depression, fear, or anger, the DNA contracted (Rein, 1996). It knotted up so that the DNA was unavailable to complete its regular functions. When one was feeling compassion, love, or gratitude, the DNA would unwind and the RNA or the messenger would then be able to access its codes and provide the natural healing of the body. Dr. Rein further found that love felt through the heart, not the mind, allows the body to regenerate its DNA to its natural state and also allows the body to heal. In addition, he found the recipient of the love also feels healing as well.

These are just a few examples of how science is proving the beneficial effects of Authentic Love, supporting the premise that we need Authentic Love to survive physically and emotionally. These benefits include:

- By experiencing Authentic Love in childhood, you will become a stable productive adult.
- Experiencing Authentic Love in adulthood, whether you had Authentic Love as a child or not, will result in a positive emotional state and help you become a stable, productive adult.
- Receiving Authentic Love as a child will result in proper brain development.
- The more you feel Authentic Love, the happier you will be.
- You will experience better health.

Spiritual Perspective

There is one thing that our great religious and modern-day spiritual teachers, such as Christ, Buddha, the Dalai Lama, Mahatma Gandhi, Krishnamurti, Mother Theresa, Louise Hay, Marianne Williamson, Gary Zukav, and Deepak Chopra, to name a few, have in common—Authentic Love. While they did/do not use the term *Authentic Love*, they exemplified, taught, and permeated Authentic Love as defined herein. They and the religions and teachings they represent, by their words and/or their actions, let us know that feeling Authentic Love is the ultimate reason why we are here on this earth.

In fact, Authentic Love is needed for our spiritual survival. We are spiritual beings having a human experience, and the main purpose of why we are having a human experience is to feel Authentic Love. We are learning this through all of our experiences—for example, forgiveness, trust, death, compassion, acceptance, tolerance, heartache, and understanding. When someone says or feels like they have profoundly learned from an experience, what they have ultimately learned is Authentic Love. This state of being, Authentic Love, where we have these feelings for ourselves, our family, and everyone in the world, is where we feel our best, at peace. We have learned through both positive and negative life experiences that Authentic Love for others and ourselves is really all that matters.

Authentic Love is also essential to our mental health as we progress through life. If we are constantly having negative feelings of hate, violence, envy, jealousy, and so on, it can lead to depression, illness, and poor mental health. We just need to put on the news, and we are bombarded with these damaging experiences and images. Believing that the world is a harmful place inevitably causes fear to set in. These negative emotions make us unhappy, and this low form of energy eventually affects our mental and physical capabilities. It takes courage, strength, and an understanding of what Authentic Love is and why we need it to break through even our adverse experiences.

We know universally, without science, that when infants aren't held, they cry even louder and eventually become despondent. We also know that when Authentic Love is not felt in children and adults, they feel something inherently missing, and it can result in all types of mental issues, such as depression, anger, discouragement, and unhappiness. No matter what age, we never stop needing Authentic Love. Marianne Williamson, in *A Return to Love*, states, "human relationships exist to produce love." She further notes that we are threatening our emotional survival when we have unloving thoughts or actions toward others and that if we don't follow the highest internal law, love, we will not survive (Williamson, 1996).

Parents must have Authentic Love for their children because their children simply exist for no other reason other than they are human beings. No conditions. Then you have the basis for stable, well-adjusted children. If the love that is given is conditional, problems with that child's internal environment, and therefore external environment, are inevitable. The child will grow up feeling unworthy as they are. They will feel that Authentic Love will only come to them if they live up to the requirements of who was supposed to have loved them as a child.

In Buddhism, the term typically used for Authentic Love is *loving kindness*, which implies compassion as well as love. Loving kindness involves wanting others to be happy. It is also unconditional and, therefore, requires immense courage, acceptance, nonattachment, and selflessness. His Holiness the Dalia Lama said, "Love and compassion are necessities, not luxuries. Without them, humanity cannot survive."[1] He also said, "All major religious traditions are basically the same message, that is love, compassion and forgiveness, the important thing is they should be part of our daily lives."[2] The Dalai Lama has been very clear in extoling the need for Authentic Love to have a thriving and joyful life.

We also need Authentic Love to reach our highest spiritual potential, collectively and individually. When we have Authentic Love, our soul blossoms and expands, allowing who we are to shine through and be. Nothing else but our Authentic Love will allow others to do the same. It will also allow us to understand others, as with Authentic Love, we are free from judgment.

Many spiritual teachers believe that Authentic Love actually brings you closer to God, the Divine, or your higher self.

> Life is love and love is life.
> —Bhagavad-Gita

Deepak Chopra, in *The Path to Love,* writes specifically that "love can bring us closer to God" (Chopra, 1998). Furthermore, in the Christian faith, the New International Version states, "Whoever does not love does not know God, because God is love" (1 John 4:8, NIV) and "God is love. Whoever lives in love, lives in God and God in them" (1 John 4:16, NIV).

Many teachers from the Hindu and Muslim faiths have exemplified that Authentic Love brings you to a higher spiritual awareness. Sai Baba, a great Indian teacher, said, "Love one another and help others to rise to higher levels, simply by pouring out love." Muhammad said, "You will never enter paradise until you have faith and you will never have faith until you love one another," and, "The best of houses is the house where the orphan gets love and kindness." In addition, Krishnamurti said, "The moment you have in your heart this extraordinary thing called love and feel the depth, the delight, the ecstasy of it, you will discover that for you the world is transformed." Mahatma Gandhi simply and importantly said, "Where there is love there is life."

Furthermore, the Vedic view believes that we are creators, as God is. Our true nature, spirit, is masked by our human existence. They also believe that it is more natural to create

Authentic Love than non-love. In the Baha'i Faith, "the love of God attracts the individual toward God, by purifying the human heart and preparing it for the revelation of divine grace." In Sikhism, Guru Gobind Singh Ji stated, "Only those who have love, will attain God," and, "When one's mind is full of love, the person will overlook deficiencies in others and accept them wholeheartedly as a product of God."

Clearly, religious and spiritual masters have shown us that Authentic Love is the spiritual path that leads us to our highest self or highest attainment. Authentic Love is needed for us to thrive and survive as spiritual beings and reach our ultimate goal.

Compassion and love are not mere luxuries. As the source both of inner and external peace, they are fundamental to the continued survival of our species.
—His Holiness the XIV Dalai Lama

4. WHAT HAPPENS WHEN I HAVE AUTHENTIC LOVE?

The Secret of Life: To Love.

WHEN YOU FEEL AUTHENTIC LOVE, there is no other feeling. It is calm, bliss, and peace—all combined. It is a sense that all is right with the world and that nothing is lacking. It is a sense of completeness and fulfillment. It allows the soul to shine forth. It allows appropriate decisions and choices to be made and to flow with life. It allows us to be free of judgment and free of the trappings of the ego.

Nothing but benefit is experienced when you feel Authentic Love. To further describe what happens when you generate Authentic Love, the following occurs:

- You become peaceful and content.
- Positive emotions (e.g., forgiveness, happiness, generosity, etc.) become easier to feel and become more prevalent.
- The world and those around you benefit from Authentic Love.
- You attract Authentic Love.

- Your energy increases.
- People want to be with you and around you.
- Negative emotions, such as grief and judgment, are released or diminished.
- You are able to face difficulties with courage.
- You see beauty everywhere.
- It connects you to your soul and the Divine.
- Eventually, Authentic Love becomes the dominant feeling.

Authentic Love transforms your life. Rhonda Byrne, in *The Secret,* writes that if you love everyone and everything and if you act and think with love, your life will be transformed. She equates the law of love with the law of attraction, and therefore, by the rules of the law of attraction, you are harnessing the greatest power, and you will attract the greatest power (Byrne, 2006).

> If you could only love enough, you could be the most powerful person in the world.
>
> — Emmet Fox

Peace and Contentment

When you feel Authentic Love, there is a profound sense of peace, contentment, and all rightness. This is the result of acting and feeling from your soul. Authentic Love allows you to act and be as your soul. "You" become your soul. Your soul, since it is connected to the Divine, is eternal and is peace. Correspondingly, you feel and have acceptance of what is, and you are operating from a space of being in the present moment, as you can only experience your soul when you are in the present moment. There is no anxiety, stress, or fear. If you can imagine what it would feel like if you had no fear or stress and lived in the present moment with acceptance of what is with an open loving heart, you will feel peace and contentment. This is what you feel when you have Authentic Love.

When you choose to have Authentic Love, you and your life are peaceful. When you choose not to have Authentic Love, you are unhappy and full of discontent, and your life can become confused, painful, and difficult. If you want to have quality of life with joy, peace, and contentment, Authentic Love is essential.

Positive Emotions Increase

Many spiritual masters have spoken the words "we become what we think." If you think positive thoughts, you become positive, as it is easier and natural to feel other positive thoughts and emotions at that time, such as compassion, forgiveness, acceptance, kindness, and non-judgment. Likewise, if you think negative thoughts, you become negative. If you think you are wonderful, loving, and lovable, you tend to act that way. If you think you are Authentic Love, you are Authentic Love. If you think you don't have Authentic Love, then you don't. Since Authentic Love is a positive state of being, your positive emotions will increase. Furthermore, Authentic Love and positive emotions are cyclic in nature. Since positive emotions help to generate Authentic Love and since Authentic Love helps with feeling positive emotions, a cycle of positivity results.

Benefits the World

When you feel Authentic Love, it benefits the world and those around you. Marianne Williamson, in *A Return to Love,* writes that when love reaches a critical mass, the world will experience a radical shift (Williamson, 1996). The radical shift will be a world where the norm is peace, nonviolence, acceptance, and compassion. Feeling Authentic Love and removing fear helps the earth and those around us. It is addressing the world's problem at its core—lack of Authentic Love. Generating Authentic Love is not a Band-Aid solution; it is a cure.

If people had enough love in their lives, there would be great respect for others. This respect would manifest in listening and wanting to understand others, resulting in conflicts being resolved as opposed to ensuing violence and war. Environmental issues would be at the top of countries' agendas, as we would love the earth and ourselves too much to allow further destruction. Famine would cease to exist, as we would help those in need. If we want the world to heal, Authentic Love is an essential element as a shift occurs in how we live our lives within and without, affecting all of those around us. We need to remove any desire or intent to harm others or the planet, and we should just want the best for everyone. If we had Authentic Love, this transition would occur.

Attracts Authentic Love

When you have Authentic Love, you attract others who have Authentic Love. There is no shortage of Authentic Love or people who have Authentic Love. Some show it more than others, but that is because they have removed the walls that have hidden it. But when you recognize and feel Authentic Love, you attract it.

I am struck by the change that happened to me when I consciously felt and gave out

> Sis vis amari, ama. If you want to be loved, love.
> — Seneca

Authentic Love to people that I met. They reacted to me with equal Authentic Love, shown through kindness, presence, and attention. Prior to consciously feeling Authentic Love, the response I got from people was mixed; some were kind, some were indifferent, and some were not kind. But when I felt Authentic Love consciously, it almost always came back.

When it didn't come back, it was due to one of two reasons. The first was when I had expectations of receiving it back, and therefore, it wasn't real Authentic Love I was sending, because it came with conditions. The second reason was because the person I was sending it to had too many walls built up as a result of their life experiences and ego to even feel or recognize Authentic Love in me or Authentic Love in themselves. Therefore, this individual was not able to reciprocate.

Increased Energy

Your heart is actually a major energy center or chakra. When you have Authentic Love, or moments of Authentic Love, your heart is actually open. This opening allows for so many other things to occur. One of these is that you are able to tap into infinite energy. Have you ever noticed that when you have "fallen in love" with someone, which initially in a new love can definitely be Authentic Love, you can stay up all night or be with your loved one all day without any sign of tiredness? When you feel Authentic Love, energy is flowing as it should, free and unencumbered by negativity or your negative stories, which cause your heart to close.

When your heart is closed caused by negative emotions or depression, you don't have energy. Typical of depression is lethargy and lack of energy. When we are in any state of our heart being closed, we lack energy. When you have Authentic Love, you are trusting and free of fear, and the walls come down, allowing free flow of energy. Watch what happens to your energy when the one that you feel Authentic Love for does something that you don't like or don't feel good about. Your heart closes, and your energy level goes down. Then watch what happens when your loved one apologizes; you feel much better, your heart opens, and energy starts flowing.

Michael Singer, in *The Untethered Soul,* states that unfinished energy patterns from your past cause the heart to be blocked (Singer, 2007). If you are constantly going over negative experiences and emotions and do not figure out why these exist and let them go, your heart will remain closed and energy will not flow.

Similarly, new experiences can elicit a variety of emotions, from fear and anger to compassion, joy, and Authentic Love, typically related to your past experiences. If the negative emotions get stuck within you, the energy cannot pass and the heart cannot open. Until you deal with these past and current negativities—that is, understand where they are coming from and why—you will not be able to let them go. This is usually, but not always, easier said than done, but this is the spiritual path. It is the way to Authentic Love.

People Want to Be Around You

Similar to attracting others who have Authentic Love, you will simply attract people. Everyone wants to feel Authentic Love, even if they do not know that Authentic Love is what they want. They just find themselves attracted to people who have Authentic Love. Think of all those great spiritual masters who have/had people follow them, even blindly. In India, Mata Amritanandamayi, also known as Amma, has so much

Authentic Love that she has hugged and comforted over thirty-four million people. She explained that a "continuous stream of love flows from me to all of creation"[1] and that this love is her inborn nature.

You will find that animals want to be around you. Animals, even wild animals, which are also sentient beings, are attracted to Authentic Love, as this is what drives all sentient beings toward Authentic Love. You never see animals around angry, hateful people. Animals want to be around people with warm, loving feelings. Children and pets, in particular, will gravitate toward you as well as other people who feel the same way or are in need of Authentic Love. Those who are closed or have a lot of negativity will tend not to be drawn to those with Authentic Love.

Assists in Releasing Negative Emotions

As previously discussed, it is impossible to feel two emotions at once. That is, you can't feel fear and Authentic Love at once. They can change from one to another quickly, but you can only feel one at a time. Therefore, when you are feeling Authentic Love, you can't feel any negative emotions. So, the more you feel Authentic Love, the less you are able to experience adverse feelings.

When you have Authentic Love, other positive emotions flow naturally. There is an easy and natural transition to positive emotions, such as compassion, acceptance, forgiveness, connection, and kindness.

When there is a conscious decision to want to feel Authentic Love more often, you also need to consciously decide to let go of negative emotions. This involves recognizing the negative emotion as soon as possible and letting it go or understanding where it is coming from and why and then letting it go. There are many ways to figure out and release adverse emotions. Some need to work on each emotion individually as they arise; others just realize that in order to feel Authentic Love more often or continually, the negative emotion just needs to be released. To do this, we see the behavior causing the negativity but don't get absorbed in it or latch onto it, which just serves the ego. When you do this, the negative emotion will float away, like a leaf on a river.

Many religions also explain how Authentic Love can help overcome negative emotions. In the *Old Path White Clouds* by Thich Nhat Hanh, he says that the Buddha taught his son Rahula to practice loving kind-

> Everyone says love hurts, but that is not true. Loneliness hurts. Rejection hurts. Losing someone hurts. Envy hurts. Everyone gets things confused with love, but in reality love is the only thing in this world that covers up all pain and makes someone feel wonderful again. Love is the only thing in this world that does not hurt.
>
> — Liam Neeson

ness to overcome anger. This results in bringing happiness to others without expecting anything else in return (Thich Nhat Hanh, 1987). His Holiness the Dalai Lama, in *The Little Book of Buddhism,* also states that if you lose the love in your mind, you will see others as enemies. Even with knowledge, education, or material wealth, you will experience suffering and confusion (His Holiness the Dalai Lama, 2000). Furthermore, in Christianity, the New International Version states, "Above all, love each other deeply, because love covers over a multitude of sins" (1 Peter 4:8, NIV).

Helps Grief

Authentic Love expands your heart to relieve pain, such as grief. Grief is the feeling of loss and helplessness, and fear is the feeling of anxiety, distress, and

> Grief can be the garden of compassion. If you keep your heart open through everything, your pain can become your greatest ally in your life's search for love and wisdom.
>
> — Rumi

concern, which are all negative emotions. As previously mentioned, since you can have only one feeling at a time, when you are in a state of Authentic Love, these negative feelings are not experienced. It is like light casting out darkness.

The last stage of grief recovery, according to the Kübler-Ross model, is acceptance. Since acceptance is a quality of Authentic Love, Authentic Love can assist in the grieving process. Additionally, typical of grief is depression and relatedly, fatigue. With moments of Authentic Love, the energy generated within the heart chakra will dissipate the fatigue, giving strength to release or offset the grief.

Reduces Judgment

Judgment is the ability to come to conclusions. However, typical of the human mind is the need to judge others whether we have the right and complete information to do so or not. It is the ego that judges to boost itself up or make itself better by pretending to know more or comparing itself to others. For this reason, judging characteristically results in negativity and false assumptions.

Authentic Love means you see Authentic Love in everybody and everything. If this is your mind-set, even intermittently, there is no need or any desire to judge or come to conclusions about others, right or wrong, or compare yourself to others. With Authentic Love, there is likewise a strong sense of acceptance of events and people, and with acceptance there is no judgment. Not judging will then benefit you for not getting trapped within negativity and false assumptions.

Able to Face Difficulties

With all of the additional positive feelings that come with or are a natural transition to Authentic Love, there is less fear and greater strength to face adversities. Acceptance is one of these emotions that actually allows you to see the difficulty as it is but not to overstress or exaggerate what is perceived as a difficulty. The energy from your heart chakra and calmness and peacefulness from feeling Authentic Love correspondingly provides the courage to deal with arising problems. It also means you don't withdrawal when things go badly but face situations as they come.

See Beauty Everywhere

When your heart is open and it feels like it is overflowing, one of the other consequences is that you perceive beauty everywhere—in someone's face, light moving through trees, or a flower. In fact, beauty is also seen in what society would deem otherwise, such as a rainbow sheen caused by gasoline on water, an old gnarled hand, or even or a smoke formation caused by fire.

The phrase "beauty is in the eye of the beholder" is used often when someone sees splendor that is generally not seen as beautiful by society. In order for the beholder to see beauty, she or he must be in a state of Authentic Love. Actual beauty cannot realistically be felt without Authentic Love in our hearts. A person with Authentic Love in his or her heart sees what is without judgment, and when there is no judgment, there is only magnificence. Likewise, in order for any type of artist (i.e., visual, auditory, and performing) to produce beautiful art, she or he must be in a state of Authentic Love. Have you ever seen beautiful art produced by anger, hate, or unworthiness? Interesting and moving art can be produced with negativity, but beauty is only produced from Authentic Love.

Connects You to Your Soul and the Divine

When you have Authentic Love in your heart and really feel it, that is your true being; you are your soul, without the trappings of your ego. When you are your soul, that is when you can connect with your higher self, the Divine, universal consciousness, God, your teachers and guides or whom and what you ultimately believe you want to connect with. Whatever you want to call it, it is all the same, and you have access to it when you have Authentic Love. Without Authentic Love, this connection is not possible.

Becomes the Dominant Feeling

Eventually, as you consciously feel Authentic Love more and more, instead of it being fleeting, it becomes the dominant feeling. How great would life be with fewer negative emotions and feeling peace, contentment, and reciprocity that come with Authentic Love? Ultimately, there will come a time when you don't need Authentic Love from others because you are completely Authentic Love.

> **Even offering three hundred bowls of food**
> **three times a day does not match the spiritual**
> **merit gained in one moment of love.**
> —Nagarjuna

5. WHAT DOES AUTHENTIC LOVE FEEL LIKE?

Wherever you are, and whatever you do, be in love.
—Rumi

AUTHENTIC LOVE CANNOT BE SEEN with the eyes, heard with the ears, or felt by the skin. However, a sight, like the smile of a baby, or a sound, like someone saying "I love you" or beautiful music that touches your soul, can be a clue to or representative of Authentic Love. Authentic Love is energy or a vibration that, therefore, cannot be felt by the senses. Authentic Love is felt in the spiritual heart by the soul.

However, some, including me, have a related physical sensation when I generate Authentic Love. I feel a slight physical sensation in my heart area, which is a feeling of expansion, openness, with a slight pressure and warmth. Others feel it through their entire body, and healers can typically feel it in their hands. Related nonphysical feelings include those of bliss, acceptance, tolerance, compassion, hope, gratitude, appreciation, trust ... all of these combined. Like nothing is wrong. When my heart is clearly closed, especially when I am hiding from hurt, I am angry, or I am feeling any other negative emotion, there is either no feeling from or an ache in my heart area.

In Ayurveda, the heart center, which is where Authentic Love is felt, is also the fourth chakra or Anahata. Anahata means "unhurt" or "unstuck," and beneath the hurt of past experience is a place where hurt does not exist. When your heart chakra is open, love, compassion, forgiveness, and acceptance flow, and when your heart chakra is closed, your heart feels anger, pain, grief, jealousy, and other negative emotions. The heart chakra is tied to emotions and love, and it is also where your power resides. If your power is hatred or Authentic Love, this is where you will feel it.

How is Authentic Love felt or known when someone feels Authentic Love for you? It can't be felt through the five senses; it needs to be perceived through your intuition. It requires a different level of perception, which is a knowing of, and by, your soul or higher self but not your ego. It is the intuitive knowledge of our hearts. If we are not connected to our hearts, we cannot perceive, feel, or give Authentic Love.

> Love is, above all else, the gift of oneself.
>
> — Jean Anouilh

Furthermore, many describe the feeling of Authentic Love as a mixture of joy, gratitude, contentment, calmness, subtle bliss, acceptance, and peace. Some feel that it is very calm and subtle, while others feel a slight sense of excitement. Others are just not able to describe the feeling; however, the smiles on their faces and the looks in their eyes make it clear that they know when someone is feeling Authentic Love for them.

We can express Authentic Love and we can experience Authentic Love through the physical by being attentive and present, conveying kind words or a smile, by giving a gift and showing compassion and joy. However, you know you have

Authentic Love when all you want for the other person or being is peace, even if it means you do not get want your ego wants, which is typically attention or love in return.

Rumi said, "Lovers don't finally meet somewhere. They were in each other all along." This guides us to the great teaching that we are all

> The minute I heard my first love story, I started looking for you, not knowing how blind that was. Lovers don't finally meet somewhere. They're in each other all along.
> — Rumi

connected; we are all one. When you have Authentic Love for another person, you experience that he or she is not separate from you. There is a closeness that is felt in which you have a feeling for the other's soul. When you look into another being's eyes and recognize that he or she is the Divine, like you, that is when you truly feel Authentic Love. That is when you are overcome with a feeling that is indescribable. However, peace and bliss are the closest words to describe this feeling of Authentic Love.

When your heart feels Authentic Love for another without knowing who they are but knowing their innermost state is the Divine and

> As long as in love there is "you" and "me", there is love not fully kindled.
> — Hazart Inayat Khan

completely recognizing equanimity and the oneness of all, you have mastered Authentic Love. That is what Authentic Love feels like; that is what Authentic Love is.

> **Love... is transcending the ego to connect with another.**
> —Joan Konner

6. HOW DO I GENERATE AUTHENTIC LOVE?

Your task is not to seek for love, but merely seek and find all the barriers within yourself that you have built against it.

—Rumi

EVERYONE IS BORN with Authentic Love. The degree to which we can express it depends on our life experiences and how much our ego is covering it. More specifically, it depends on how strong the ego is, which is directly correlated to the amount someone shows and feels Authentic Love.

There are situations, comfortable limited situations, where we find it easy to generate Authentic Love. Typically, this occurs when, and with whom, we feel safe. Wouldn't it be wonderful to feel safe in every relationship and circumstance where we can generate Authentic Love?

> Pain doesn't stem from the love we're denied from others, but rather from the love that we deny them.
>
> —*A Return to Love* by Marianne Williamson

There is the belief that where we came from before we were born and where we go when we die, in other words, the afterlife, is a place where we feel Authentic Love continuously.

Which, therefore, would be a place of great peace, bliss, and calmness. This, and the resulting feelings of Authentic Love in this existence, is what we are searching for. So, instead of "How do I generate Authentic Love?" the better question may be "How do I get my internal Authentic Love back?"

Generating Authentic Love is a choice and can occur voluntarily or involuntarily. It is felt through and generated by our spiritual heart or soul but can have some consequential related physical sensations. Authentic Love is generated when our negative emotions are not currently present and we don't have any conditions or attachment to that feeling of love.

There is the belief that you need something negative in your life to happen in order to grow or come to Authentic Love. That you need to become ill or have a loved one die or be in pain for one to realize what really matters. For some, positive emotions and Authentic Love are realized when negative experiences and emotions are too difficult to deal with; therefore, energetically they have to let go of the negative feelings to stop the pain. Positive emotions are then able to come forth. Hazrat Inayat Khan said, "God breaks the heart again and again and again until it stays open." For many people, their heart breaks and breaks until they realize what Authentic Love is. Until they keep their heart open and generate Authentic Love, it will continue to break and feel broken.

But this path from negativity to Authentic Love is not always necessary. You can choose to grow spiritually and choose to feel and practice Authentic Love without any negative experiences to compel you to feel Authentic Love. You just have to do it.

Actions to Generate Authentic Love

Like a muscle, love can be strengthened through practice. There are numerous actions that can be put into practice to generate Authentic Love. Not all of these will ring true for you, so pick which ones appeal to you and then practice those. When these actions become mastered or if they are not working as well for you as they had been in the past, go back to the actions you passed over and determine which ones work for you now. Since we change on the path to Authentic Love, so will the actions that support and assist us.

Practice is extremely important to train the emotional mind and tame the ego. Like any action where results are sought, commitment to completing the actions is also necessary to receive the ultimate benefits. I have followed these actions and realized amazing results on my ability to generate Authentic Love.

While all of the actions explained here will assist in generating Authentic Love, there are two actions that are universal to generating Authentic Love: practice positive emotions and work on understanding and releasing negative emotions. In order to practice these two actions, we need to know our emotions.

Action #1: Know Your Emotions

In order to generate Authentic Love and know if you are feeling Authentic Love, you simply must know what you are feeling. You need to know your emotions. For many of us, this is difficult. We did not grow up looking at or understanding what we were feeling. For most families as in mine, we did not discuss our emotions at the dinner table, nor did we learn this in school.

The good news is that you can learn to know your emotions. It just takes practice, and the time to reflect on how you feel is needed. Start by asking yourself simple questions throughout the day: Do I feel happy, angry, jealous, confused, at peace? Initially, it might not be clear what you are feeling, but if you keep asking and making the conscious effort, you will come to understand what emotion you are experiencing.

If you reflect on what event just happened, this can lead you to understanding what emotion you are feeling. For example, if you just finished meditating, you are more than likely feeling calm, or if you have just finished an argument, you may be feeling angry, confused, or sad.

The ego can trick you into thinking that you are feeling something when you are not. You could be convinced that you are happy that your girlfriend broke up with you, when deep down you are very sad. Sometimes you may unearth one feeling to find another. With this same example, you could be experiencing anger on the surface but underneath you are feeling rejected. Sometimes you need to continue with the exploration of how you are feeling to get to the root of your emotions. You may feel betrayed if your partner has cheated on you, but you may then find that you have a fear of being alone.

Once you have a grasp of what emotions you are experiencing, you can recognize and perpetuate the positive emotions and work on releasing the negative ones.

Action #2: Foster Positive Emotions

Inspiring and influencing all positive emotions is characteristic of Authentic Love. You can have these emotions but not necessarily have Authentic Love. However, these emotions can facilitate Authentic Love and can result from expressing

Authentic Love. Therefore, by practicing, using, generating, and tapping into these positive emotions, Authentic Love will be more easily, readily, and/or actually felt and vice versa.

> We are not held back by the love we didn't receive in the past but by the love we're not extending in the present.
>
> —*A Return to Love* by Marianne Williamson

Positive emotions include, for example, compassion, forgiveness, acceptance, patience, gratitude, tolerance, kindness, patience, peace, joy, serenity, inspiration, awe, creativity, cheerfulness, and pleasantness. There are many ways to feel these positive emotions, and many of you are already practicing them. It is a conscious effort to become a better person, and in order to do this, you need to express positive emotions to more people under various circumstances. This, for instance, can include being particularly kind or accepting even when you don't agree with someone. For some, of course, it is and has become natural to feel positive emotions. If it is not quite as natural as you would like, it will need a greater conscious effort and commitment to feel these positive emotions on a regular basis.

Greater conscious effort should start with the intention to want to feel positive emotions. The intent needs to be practical, which includes feeling these positive emotions more often but not constantly, because as human beings, our emotions change, and we can't feel one specific emotion continuously. You should also expect to feel negative emotions, which is completely normal.

Intentions and affirmations are ways toward obtaining what you want. If you are not already feeling Authentic Love, you are questioning whether you are feeling Authentic Love, or you would like to feel Authentic Love more, an intention could be that "each day I will feel more Authentic Love." This alleviates the pressure of perfection and immediate results, making any progress encouraging rein-forcement.

These affirmations and intentions should be stated every morning to start the day, declaring how you want the day to unfold. When you start seeing results, you can increase your intention to feeling these positive emotions during, for example, difficult moments. Your intention could be, "May the trigger for Authentic Love be when I feel _____." (Fill in the blank with, for example, anger, fear, or jealousy). For me, I have used the word "pain," whether it was emotion or physical pain. Sure enough over time, when I would feel pain, I would remember to turn my heart to Authentic Love.

Every day, I start by writing my intentions for that day in my journal. These include, for example, keep my heart open and feel Authentic Love. Some days, my intentions are specific, and they can vary from day to day, but they always include these two intentions. Make your intentions what you feel is right for you and don't hesitate to change these inten-tions as you grow.

It is also important to recognize that you may not feel kindness and compassion all the time; nevertheless, what is important is that you are committed to these emotions being a large part of your life. There may be times when you are chal-lenged, like the person on the bus is yelling into their cell phone or your boss is angry because you are late with a deliv-erable. With the proper intent and follow-through, positive outcomes will be realized.

When dealing with difficult situations with others, I find it helpful to think, know, and see these individuals as being part of the Divine—to focus on their virtues or just think of them as a human being just like me. This usually deflates the diffi-cult situation, at least for me, and in turn I generate positive emotions and Authentic Love. Your choice of thoughts, even during challenging circumstances, creates the quality of your relationship with others.

Real change and transformation come from consciousness -- being conscious of your emotions and intentions. Changing your consciousness can occur, but it takes practice and commitment. You need to devote your time and energy to positive emotions and Authentic Love. Once you do this and others see the benefits of Authentic Love, others will follow until there is real transformation in the world.

Action #3: Managing Negative Emotions

When negative emotions, such as anger, pride, jealousy, or hatred, are felt, one of two things is occurring. The first is the feeling of fear, and the second is judgment. Fear underlies negativity because we don't understand what is going on or the situation hasn't or isn't going the way we want it. Our ego then responds with fear because of uncertainty or not knowing or understanding the circumstances surrounding the situation. Our ego requires control in order to get what it wants.

Fear is not something that we are born with. Children are typically fearless, expressing themselves without trepidation, meeting new experiences with courage and enthusiasm, and acting without worrying what people may think. It is through experiences that we learn fear. We were told: not to touch certain things in case we hurt ourselves; be careful what you say in case someone is offended and/or doesn't like you; not to eat certain foods because they are unhealthy; don't talk to strangers because they may hurt you; or not to wish for certain things in case they don't come true.

Many of us also manage to develop fears, which result in feeling negative emotions. This includes a fear of not being loved, resulting in anger and/or hatred; fear of failure, resulting in pride; fear of rejection, resulting in sadness; fear of not getting what we want, resulting in worry; fear of what one has done in the past, resulting in guilt, shame, and/or regret; fear of not having what others have, resulting in jealously and/or envy; and so on. All of these fears have a further consequence of additional fears, such as a fear of hurting oneself or others or of not getting a desired outcome. Even behaviors are the cause of some form of fear, including, for example, manipulation, cruelty, and condescension.

The second underlying emotion to negativity is judgment. In difficult situations, a negative reaction is created as the situation is being judged as undesirable. This then can act as a trigger to a negative emotion, which is actually reflective of something related to what is going on inside of you, not the person or situation you are having the adversity with. For example, anger may result when someone is trying to help you, but because you have the internal need to do things on your own and prove yourself, you get angry. You are judging the situation as undesirable when the other person has the best intentions.

When you have a negative emotion, you are actually acting in the absence of Authentic Love. What is causing the absence of Authentic Love and the reflective negative emotion inside of you is your path. This is what you need to understand to grow into Authentic Love.

To manage your negative emotions, you need to develop a relationship with yourself. You need to clear out the issues in your heart and mind that are causing the barriers to Authentic Love. In doing so, you need to understand the causes and conditions of negative emotions. As human beings, we cannot completely rid ourselves of negative emotions, but we can manage them. Many believe that Jesus and Buddha reached enlightenment by not allowing any emotion, negative or positive, to guide their life. What is left after the emotions is Authentic Love. Many aspire to reach enlightenment and believe that enlightenment is our ultimate goal as human beings.

To illustrate how to understand the causes and conditions of negative emotions and to show that the negative emotion is due to one's inner state, the following is an example. During family visits, my friend Julia found herself getting angry for no obvious reason, or for the most minor reasons. There was no compassion, understanding, or Authentic Love on her part, just anger. For the longest time, this scenario kept playing out, and Julia kept blaming her family, but she realized that the anger was illogical. There was no real reason in the situations that would cause one to become annoyed. She then sought to find the real reason for her anger. She meditated on it and asked to receive the actual cause for this anger. What came to her was how she felt as a child. She felt unloved and unwanted. In the present, however, some members of her family were showing her Authentic Love and support, but she was dealing with the past. It wasn't her family's actions in the present that were to blame for how she felt now; it was Julia. Not letting go of the past and an absence of Authentic Love in her heart was the cause of her anger toward her family.

Gary Zukav, in *The Seat of the Soul*, states that when we are experiencing negative emotions, it is bringing awareness to the parts of the soul that need healing (Zukav, 2007). Therefore, the presence of negative emotions is a guide on the path to uncover our souls. Gary Zukav goes on further to state that because the negative emotions are illusions, they do not actually exist. It is Authentic Love that exists.

Ralph Waldo Emerson said, "The love you withhold is the pain that you carry." Not only is Authentic Love necessary in order to deal with pain or painful situations and negative conditions, but managing negative emotions is necessary to subsequently generate Authentic Love. If you are filled with harmful emotions, there is no room for Authentic Love. Managing your negative emotions does not mean that you need to eliminate negative emotions, as this is impossible. We are human beings, and as part of our existence, we experience negative emotions. We need to, however, diminish the frequency and strength of harmful emotions over us.

Decreasing our destructive emotions also involves increasing our positive emotions, as discussed in the section above. As aptly put by Marianne Williamson, in *A Return to Love*, she compares darkness and light with fear and love. Darkness cannot be eliminated by physical means; it needs light. Likewise, eradicating fear requires love (Williamson, 1996).

Many of our harmful emotions are self-inflicted and self-deprecating. If you had Authentic Love for yourself, identical to, for example, the Authentic Love you have for your children, you would remove some of the barriers to healing. When you have Authentic Love for yourself, you will: have patience, not expect perfection; not feel guilt or shame for something that you did; and have forgiveness for yourself. This will thereby decrease many of the negative emotions and increase the positive emotions, bringing you to Authentic Love or at least closer to Authentic Love.

Releasing harmful emotions and the negative consequences of those emotions, such as attracting more adverse emotions within yourself or from others, can be done by changing your behavior. By recognizing these emotions and consciously changing them to positive thoughts and emotions about the situation, whether they are or not, can change the consequences. To illustrate this, the following is a personal example with my dog, Obi. Obi is a very cute and headstrong miniature schnauzer. He would often get into trouble, usually by stealing things and chewing them. No matter how many times I said no and made him sit in his corner, he would do the very same action again, again, and again. I started labeling him a "bad dog" and had negative feelings about his behavior. The negative behavior continued. I then realized what I had been taught: negative behavior and negative reinforcement attract negative behavior. I put the opposite into practice and started feeling more Authentic Love toward him, feeling that he was good dog and telling him and others that he was a good dog. I also started not getting angry with him for his bad behavior and just calmly removed what he was not to have. He then started actually acting like a good dog. What a lesson.

What I found was that I needed to do a lot of work in order for Authentic Love to be uncovered. For me, it has taken time, and the process continues. I make a point of always checking in to understand exactly what I am feeling. Whatever the emotion, I examine why I am feeling that emotion. Some emotions have a deep inner meaning, such as when I spend time just talking with my son, I have a feeling of inner peace. Others are not so profound, like the happiness I feel when I find a good bargain on a needed pair of shoes. When I feel a negative emotion, I try to figure out why I have that emotion so that it does not become all-consuming and stay with me for a long period of time. When I am driving, I tend to get stressed and angry when there is traffic or when someone is not driving well. The reason I feel the anger is because in traffic I am not in control, which I like to be, and when someone is not driving well, I judge them to be selfish and not care about others. Whether the latter is true or not, when I come to this conclusion that I am being judgmental and I don't know their story, I realize the inappropriateness of judging and I then release the associated negative emotion of anger. I also realize that the selfishness is inside of me, not them. I am being self-ish, as I want the drive to go my way, and I want people to drive the way I think they should.

Some may say that this process is too difficult, too stressful, and too time-consuming; however, if this is what needs to be done to release something that does not feel good and is not good for you, and this brings you closer to Authentic Love, isn't it worth it? With practice, it will take less and less time. The results, even the small ones, are well worth it.

Examining and managing emotions, both the positive and negative emotions, is a spiritual path. This emotional aware-ness is essential for any spiritual development. Everyone's path is different, so the examination into the emotions can take the form of individual exploration, with assistance by a teacher or guru, through interactions with people, from wisdom in related books, or any combination of these. Your emotions are signals to what you must work on to understand why you are feeling the way you are feeling. This provides insight into managing your emotions and opening the way for Authentic Love.

Action #4: Practice Forgiveness

Not forgiving is one of the main hindrances to feeling Authentic Love. When you need to forgive, something clearly damaging has occurred that you feel negativity toward and are not able to let go of it. With this, usually many negative emotions are trapped, such as anger, resentment, hurt, and betrayal toward another or even yourself. All of these negative emotions are stopping you from feeling Authentic Love.

Forgiveness is a very active process in terms of under-standing and being conscious of one's feelings and thoughts.

In order to forgive, we must practice positive thoughts to those we want to forgive. Neither indifferent thoughts and emotions nor negative thoughts and emotions will bring out forgiveness. As another personal example, there was a woman that I worked with for several years who clearly did not like me. She made her feelings toward me very clear and would say negative, hurtful things about me to many people at work. She was a person that I did not have loving thoughts toward to begin with, but I soon began to resent her and have anger toward her. Knowing that I needed to forgive her to release my negative emotions and thoughts, I realized that Authentic Love had to come into play in order to forgive.

True and complete forgiveness cannot come about without feeling Authentic Love for a person. Partial forgiveness can be felt when we no longer feel anger or we feel indifference toward that person. But for real forgiveness to occur, Authentic Love needs to be felt. So it was very difficult to generate Authentic Love for someone that I hadn't felt those emotions toward before the negative actions had occurred. My Authentic Love for her came in the form of feeling Authentic Love for all human beings. We are human beings, and for that reason alone, we deserve Authentic Love. She is not just the negative behavior that she exhibits, and she has a soul just as beautiful as mine. Generating Authentic Love for all without all of the conditions and trappings of my ego and experiences, coupled with letting go of the past to, therefore, not ruin the present or future is what allowed and facilitated my forgiveness to occur.

Forgiveness can typically occur much easier for those you have previously had Authentic Love for. Remembering the previous loving thoughts and

> To forgive is merely to remember only the loving thoughts you gave in the past, and those that were given you. All the rest must be forgotten.
>
> — *A Course in Miracles*

letting go of the actions that
created the need for forgiveness will allow forgiveness to
materialize. Forgiveness cannot occur without feelings of
Authentic Love and letting go of the past actions -- yours and
theirs.

There are many books showing many ways that can help
achieve forgiveness. Many include confronting the person that
you need to forgive and letting them know from your perspective how you feel. If you cannot face the person or do not want
to face the person, you can write them and then recite the
letter as if they were there. The next step is to throw the letter
out in the garbage or burn the letter. The reciting and burning
act as a metaphorical release for letting it go and achieving
forgiveness.

Jack Canfield, in *The Success Principles,* has very practical
exercises in realizing forgiveness (Canfield, 2005). Success
Principle No. 29 - Complete the Past to Embrace the Future,
proposes six steps to forgiveness, which includes acknowledging the resentment, pain, and resulting fears and self-
doubts and acknowledging your role in the event occurring. It
also involves putting yourself in the other's shoes to try to
understand the circumstances that led to the event. Then
finally, letting it go and forgiving the person.

Action #5: Presence and Attention Are Needed

Generating Authentic Love is only possible when it is done in
the present moment. Being in the present moment allows you
to put conscious attention on expressing Authentic Love in an
action or in a situation or to a being. The present moment is
where our true nature, or soul, lies and can be tapped into.
When you are thinking about the past or future, which does
not exist in the present, you cannot reach your soul. Further-

more, when you tap into your soul in the present moment, your ego cannot exist. The ego wants you to be in the past or future to focus on thoughts that take you away from the present, to take you outside of what is actually happening in the now.

Unblocking the heart to feel Authentic Love requires putting your attention on your heart. Working on opening the heart requires a conscious effort. Should your heart open briefly, you need to pay attention to this so that you can recognize it and understand the causes and effects of feeling what it is like to have your heart open. This too can only be felt if you are in the present moment. If the mind is in the future or the past, you will miss the experience. Therefore, presence and attention are needed in the present moment for Authentic Love to occur.

Throughout the day, ask yourself the question: where is my mind—in the past, present, or future? Regardless of the answer, by asking the question, you are bringing your thoughts into the present, as you are asking where your mind is in the present moment. All you have to do is ask the question.

Action #6: Need to Feel Lovable

You need to feel lovable to have and attract Authentic Love. If you feel you are not deserving of Authentic Love, then you will not receive it and you will not be able to generate it. You cannot have feelings of Authentic Love for yourself when you are too busy feeling that you are not deserving. Feelings of being lovable or unlovable can stem from childhood or from our current culture. Our current culture views feeling lovable as a selfish, egocentric quality, when in fact feeling lovable is a spiritual quality.

Like attracts like, and therefore, if you feel you are not lovable, you will attract further feelings of not being lovable. You will also attract people who are not loving and experiences that are not loving. As you demonstrate Authentic Love toward others, these occurrences result in yet a deeper feeling of Authentic Love, which extends to yourself. You then feel lovable and are more lovable.

For me, loving myself and knowing that I am lovable did not come easily. It finally came to me when I had the following realization: to help feel lovable, recognize that whatever your upbringing was, whatever you have experienced throughout your life and whatever you are experiencing in the present moment, you are a beautiful human being. The Divine, God, and spiritual masters, no matter who you are, recognize your divinity, and therefore you are worthy of your love and love from others. How can they be wrong?

Action #7: Consciousness and Choice

For some people or under certain circumstances, Authentic Love is generated automatically or involuntarily. For others or under other situations, a decision to open your heart to generate Authentic Love is required. Once there is a deliberate decision that you want to have Authentic Love, you need to consciously decide to open your heart. This conscious decision is made with your mind. Without your heart and mind on board, Authentic Love will not be felt.

The automatic or involuntary feeling of Authentic Love can typically come from, for example, being in the presence of a baby, child, pet, or partner. To those who feel they have not and cannot generate Authentic Love, you will, and it just takes practice. It may require specific conditions for you to grow and generate the conditions to feel Authentic Love, but rest assured, it is who we are. We all have the potential. When on the path, it is not a matter of if, but when.

During spiritual growth, there is always a time when we choose peace, joy, and love. We recognize that we do not want negative emotions; we want positive emotions because of how they make us feel. The highest frequencies make us feel the best, make us feel full of energy, confidence, and positivity. We choose positive emotions and Authentic Love.

The consciousness and choice toward the positive emotions and, in particular, Authentic Love will result in meeting the needs of your soul and the reason why you are having this human existence. Each of our lives takes different paths, and the needs of your soul in the physical existence can be different from others; however, when you infuse it with positive emotions and Authentic Love, then you know you are on the right path.

When you have a conscious transformation to the higher-frequency emotions and energy, you will naturally be connected to your higher self, the universe, the Divine, or God. This consciousness allows you to be cognizant of the present moment and the signs and information from these entities. Without consciousness of your higher vibrations, you cannot connect with your higher self, the universe, the Divine, or God.

Facilitating consciousness and choice involves making a commitment and revisiting that commitment. The commitment can be in the form of a pledge to choose Authentic Love, which can be done in writing or verbally. Commitments are not to be taken lightly. For me, I write that I will feel Authentic Love in my journal every morning. Whichever way you choose and the frequency of making this promise will allow for the commitment to be embedded in your heart and mind.

Action #8: Open Your Heart

Having an open heart is necessary for spiritual growth and for you to be open to people and the situations around you. Some feel a physical sensation of openness and expansion in the area of the heart when Authentic Love is generated. We have all felt the heart swell with love and ache when hurt. However, the painful sensations are felt when your heart is closed. Furthermore, when you have shut down your emotions, you don't even feel your heart. A closed heart cannot feel Authentic Love or even feel positive emotions for that matter.

Even though your physical heart cannot be opened, there is a physical-ness to opening your spiritual heart. When I open my heart, I feel it as an actual opening sensation coupled with pressure and warmth. We have

> Closing our hearts destroys our peace because it's alien to our nature. It warps us and turns us into people we're not meant to be.
>
> — *A Return to Love* by Marianne Williamson

all felt the swelling of the heart when love is felt. The best way to recognize this feeling is to contemplate someone you love. Think of them in front of you wanting to show them how much you have Authentic Love for them but without saying or doing anything. Sometimes it helps if you see them in distress or at a point where they need love. This then elicits compassion as well as Authentic Love, which allows you to unwrap your heart and feel the sensation of opening your heart.

If you are worried that if you open your heart you may get hurt, rest assured, no one can hurt you if you understand and have Authentic Love. No one can truly hurt you unless you let them. Barriers around the heart do not generate love; they generate fear. This was a big revelation for me, as I had many layers of walls built up throughout my life. Every once in a while, when I felt safe, I would experience the feeling of opening my heart. Then I tried it under less safe conditions and then under not safe conditions, and you know what? I was not hurt because my heart was open and filled with Authentic Love. When it is filled with Authentic Love, it cannot feel anything else, least of all hurt or pain.

Physical exercise, in particular specific heart opening yoga positions, coupled with conscious intent to open the heart can actually help open your heart. One of these movements involves sitting on your knees with your rear on your heels or just sitting on a chair. With a straight back, start with your hands in the prayer posture level with your heart, elbows down. Then push your arms straight out until the palms open out straight in front of you. Next, extend the arms out your side parallel to the ground, extending out from your shoulders. Then bring the arms back out in front of you with palms extended out. Place the palms together and then bring your arms and hands back to prayer posture. Now do this several more times and while doing this, consciously feel the energy of your hands pulling the energy of your heart out, which brings the energy out from your heart. This actually opens your heart.

Action # 9: To Receive, You Must Give

To receive Authentic Love, you must give Authentic Love. As previously discussed, Authentic Love is the law of attraction. When you feel Authentic Love and infuse what you do with Authentic Love, you will receive Authentic Love and you will receive more of whatever you are doing. If you are being generous, you will receive more generosity.

Have you ever met someone who is constantly complaining about not having enough money and yet they never have enough money? What you focus on and where your attention goes, you will create. This is true for both posi-tive and negative intentions. So, you must practice giving Authentic Love as often as possible. Make this a daily practice and promise. Start by making the commitment to consciously feel Authentic Love to one person during the day and make note of who this was either at the end of the day or the next morning when you are making another commitment. By committing to writing this down, you are becoming account-able to yourself. Increase the number of people per day as the weeks progress until you generate Authentic Love to everyone you meet.

Action #10: Meditate

When your mind is still and, therefore, your ego is quiet, that is when you can also feel Authentic Love. When the mind is calm, Authentic Love is what is left. Meditation is a way to still the mind. During meditation, the idea is to watch your thoughts, and when they come in, do not become attached and follow them but let them go. By not grasping onto all of your thoughts and emotions, you are making room and time for Authentic Love.

There are several types of meditation, such as shamatha, vipassana, and transcendental. Shamatha meditation is a Buddhist practice where one performs single-pointed medita-tion, most commonly through mindfulness breathing. That is, when sitting in meditation, one focuses on the breath. When the mind wanders and this is recognized, you bring your focus back to the breath. When a thought is realized, let it go. Do not go with it and all of its' stories. Take a step back and watch it flow past, like a leaf on a river.

Vipassana meditation is similar to shamatha. It, too, is a practice in the Buddhist tradition with the aim of achieving insight into the true nature of reality. This is also accomplished through focusing on the breath with mindfulness coupled with contemplation and introspection. This practice ultimately brings you to Authentic Love, which is the true nature of reality.

Transcendental meditation comes from the Vedic tradition in which one avoids distracting thoughts and brings one to a state of relaxed awareness. It involves the use of a mantra, which is recited twice per day for fifteen to twenty minutes. In order to receive the specialized mantra, once must receive it from a certified transcendental meditation teacher. The relaxed state of awareness will result in experiencing Authentic Love.

It is best to find the meditation process that is best for you. However, the following is a universal method. To begin meditating, it is recommended to start with five minutes and then gradually increase to at least twenty minutes per sitting. Meditating when you first wake up in the morning and/or just before you go to bed is ideal. You don't have to sit on a cushion cross-legged, as meditation can be done in a chair just as effectively. The key is to have your spine straight, no slouching. This will allow for the free flow of energy. Place your hands calmly on your lap. You can either have your eyes closed or downcast. The latter is helpful if you find yourself falling asleep. Focus on the feeling of the breath through the nose, and when thoughts come in, recognize them as just thoughts and bring your focus back to your breath.

By following a meditation process, eventually what is felt is a sense of clarity and nonattachment in which Authentic Love can shine through. The length of time it takes to get to this stage is dependent on the individual. It is recommended, especially if difficulties occur, that a teacher be sought to help you through the technique and various stages of meditation.

But whatever method you choose, don't get discouraged if thoughts continually come in and you are not able to achieve a peaceful mind. For many, it takes time, and thoughts coming in continuously is natural. For me I have good days where I can calm my mind quickly and easily and bad days where it is next to impossible. However, like any new activity, continual practice is needed to be successful.

Action #11: Abandon False Notions

We all have many false notions or beliefs, as our reality is based on experience and perception, which varies from person to person. One event can result in many different opinions of what actually happened. Likewise, many believe that we are limited in our capacity to love, that our past and current experiences are responsible for our ability to feel love and experience love. This belief is a false notion.

As human beings, we have the capacity to show, feel, and be Authentic Love. There are numerous examples of people who have overcome what could be perceived as imposed-upon experiences limiting the capacity to love. One of these examples was a lady whose son was murdered. Over time, she forgave her son's killer and eventually let him into her own house when he was released from prison. She did this to help him have a brighter and better future, exemplifying Authentic Love. We are all capable of this Authentic Love.

> Restoring the spiritual dimension to love means abandoning the notion of a limited self with its limited ability to love and regaining the Self with its unbounded ability to love.
> —*The Path to Love* by Deepak Chopra

One of our greatest false notions is related to our separateness. Many of us believe that we are each separate entities with no obvious connection to those around us, in our cities, and on our planet, let alone those who have come before or after our existence. Anita Moorjani, in her book *Dying to be Me*, explains that during her near-death experience, she clearly realized that we are not separate, but our souls are one with each other and the Divine (Moorjani, 2012). She describes her "infinite self" as being "one with every single thing." She further goes on to explain that this illusion of separation is caused by being too strongly identified with our external state, as opposed to our internal state.

Many of the great religions and spiritual traditions have also said that we are "one," that we are not separate from one another. What feelings we have actually affect everyone and everything else. When this feeling of oneness is clearly felt and known, it results in the feeling of Authentic Love for all. Authentic Love then becomes natural for those that we are connected to, which is everyone.

Another false notion is that we are somehow different from and inferior to the Divine. We are the Divine. If we are all one with the great spiritual masters, including Jesus and Buddha, then we are Jesus and Buddha. Our souls are one with these great masters, so we have that very nature that made them great. Once this is recognized, nothing but Authentic Love shines through us.

Contemplate these notions and beliefs yourself to determine the truth. In addition, when faced with difficulties, determine if they are caused by false notions that you have been identifying as truth. An example could be that you blame your parents for not making you feel lovable and therefore you cannot maintain a relationship because you feel unlovable. If this belief is untrue, release it, and the challenging situation will resolve itself.

Action #12: Don't Rush

You can't rush feeling Authentic Love. By rushing, you are trying to get to something or get somewhere. Authentic Love is not somewhere. It is within you. It just needs to be realized. Realization cannot be rushed. You can capture Authentic Love moment by moment, not sometime in the future to find it somewhere. If you rush, frustration will ensue, which will not allow Authentic Love to be felt.

Action #13: Identify with Your Spiritual Nature

The need to identify with your spiritual nature may be obvious, but let's be explicit. You need to identify with your spiritual nature because your soul is pure love, Authentic Love. You must identify with the nonphysical nature of your existence through the physical nature of your existence. This physical experience, through the body and mind, is allowing you the opportunity to feel and realize Authentic Love.

Identifying with your spiritual nature is understanding what is not your ego. Your ego is what causes suffering, discontent, jealousy, pride, and a whole host of other harmful emotions. It causes you to act selfishly. Identifying with your spiritual nature is the goal of the spiritual path, to find out what exists when your ego is quiet.

Quieting the mind and ego through meditation will allow you to identify with your spiritual nature. A conscious determination of whether your intentions, speech, and actions are from the ego can be accomplished by asking the following questions:

Were my intentions, speech and/or actions:

1. a) selfish or b) selfless?

2. a) based on a desired outcome or b) for the good of all?

3. a) manipulation or intent to hurt or b) understanding the truth of the situation?

If, in these examples, a) was your answer to any of these questions, then you are operating from the ego. If b) was your answer to any of these questions, then you are operating from the soul.

Action #14: See Authentic Love as a Realization

Authentic Love is not something that we acquire only through specific conditions. It is not something that is available only to a few. It is something that we all have, and upon realization of this, it then shines through. It is always there. It is just covered up. So, for some, letting go of our resistance to feeling Authentic Love will result in realizing that Authentic Love is within us. Furthermore, meditation and contemplation on what is truly in your heart will facilitate the realization.

Action #15: Release Restraint and Moderation

If you are trying to generate Authentic Love but have feelings of restriction or moderation, you will not be able to feel Authentic Love. Authentic Love is expansive and ultimately is not about control or restraint, which have a tone of fear and lack of confidence, which is on the negative side of the emotions. Positive emotions with an open heart are required to feel Authentic Love.

When you feel restrictions or restraint, the heart is closed and there is a tension associated with trying to open your heart. There is probably a fear of being hurt or you have not completely let go of what caused your heart to close. Try heart-opening exercises, as described in Action #8: Open Your Heart, along with the understanding that no one can hurt you unless you let them and that letting go will release the pain and will remove the feelings of restraint and moderation. These actions and understandings will also allow for a relaxation of the heart, which will release the tension and facilitate Authentic Love.

Action #16: Do What Makes You Feel Good

Go toward and do more of what makes you feel good. Your genuine feelings of happiness are the Divine's way of letting you know you are on the right path. When you do things you enjoy, you are on the course to positive emotions and Authentic Love. This is why so many people search to find their passion or search for what they are supposed to do with their lives, because we instinctively know this is beneficial to us.

However, sometimes the ego tricks us, and what we think makes us feel good is not really good for us. Eating a huge meal and finding money and keeping it are examples of what could make you feel good but actually doesn't. You feel sick or gain excess weight if you eat too much, and keeping something that is not yours is akin to stealing. Sometimes a feeling of superiority and greed can be perceived as pleasurable, so you need to be clear as to what you are feeling and why. You need to be diligent in understanding what you are actually feeling.

Similarly, you should not do what does not make you feel good. If it doesn't make you feel good, negative emotions, such as guilt and regret, will result. If being with an old friend makes you feel inferior or lack confidence, you need to examine whether the relationship is worth continuing. If your compulsive buying brings you temporary satisfaction but then fills you with guilt, the behavior causing the guilt needs to be modified.

This exercise of doing what makes you feel good and not doing what doesn't make you feel good is dependent on you clearly understanding your feelings. You won't get it right every time; it takes practice by reflecting on how you are feeling. Practice helps us understand and learn in order to really see and feel things the way they are and what is best for you and your path. Add commitment and courage and you are on your way to finding out what makes you feel good. When you feel good, positive emotions are more easily felt, which will allow you to experience Authentic Love.

Action #17: Listen to Your Intuition

Your intuition or gut feeling is essentially that voice or feeling that provides guidance or conveys information that does not come as a result of thought or ego, but from your higher self or soul. It may support your thoughts or not. Some say they feel it from their body, in the stomach or heart, and then it moves into their mind as opposed to coming straight from their mind. Your intuition may be helping you make a decision, providing guidance on your next steps, or giving you information about someone or a situation.

In order to tell if what you are receiving is your intuition, you need to answer the following question: Did I have a thought process directly related to what came in? That is, was what came in a logical conclusion to a thought process? If the answer is yes, then the information came from your ego. If the answer did come from your ego, that does not make it wrong; it just lets us know the origin. If the answer is no, the information came from your intuition. Your intuition provides messages from your soul. These messages, therefore, are coming from and guiding you to Authentic Love.

To illustrate how to determine if the information is coming from the soul or ego, the following is an example. When on a first date, you feel fear and you hear "Don't go home with this man." In order to determine if your intuition is warning you, first ask this question: do I normally have this fear? A fear of spiders is an example of typically having a fear. A habitual fear is not coming from your intuition. So, if your answer is "I do not normally have this fear of men when on dates," then ask yourself, "Did I have a similar thought process before the fear came in, such as 'my mother used to tell me horror stories about women who went home with men'?" Your thought process continues with, "I remember that one story was particularly scary, but then my friend said, 'Don't live your life in fear or you won't get anywhere,' but then this guy seems really nice, but ..." Then the fear came in from your ego. I am not saying that you don't listen to your ego or that your ego is wrong, just that it is not from your intuition or soul.

Another example of your intuition coming in can occur when buying a gift for someone. Have you ever just felt you needed to buy something for someone for no reason? You can either listen to it or justify not buying it. One year around Christmas, I was walking through Canadian Tire and saw a wind-up radio which does not run on batteries or electricity. I didn't know why, but I felt I needed to buy one for my father, so I did. Then I thought that I could use one of these as well, in case we ever lost power. At Christmas, when my dad opened his gift, he had a funny smile on his face and handed me my gift from him. It was the very same radio. He told me that when he bought me the radio, he wanted one as well. These gifts, while they seemed small, meant so much and came from our intuition or our souls in a place of Authentic

Love. It further made us feel connected, which allowed Authentic Love to flow.

Action #18: Align Your Ego with Your Soul

Your ego is a part of you that is covering up your soul. What it does and how it reacts is based on your life experiences and how you have interpreted and dealt with these experiences. Your ego expresses itself through your thoughts and actions and as such can cause you difficulty. When you are able to calm the mind and manage your thoughts and emotions, you are aligning your ego with your soul. When your ego is aligned and serves your soul, your ego can be very beneficial. It helps you with daily life decisions and reflects the emotions that are necessary for life and human interactions. For example, a degree of pride in your work may help you get your dream job, or tenacity may get the love of your life.

When your ego serves your soul and therefore does not conceal it, Authentic Love will shine through. Your ego, then, does not spend its time causing problems and covering up your soul. Aligning your ego with your soul can be achieved through the same process of generating Authentic Love. Since we as human beings cannot get rid of the ego, controlling your thoughts and the intentions of your thoughts and actions brings the ego in line with the soul.

Gary Zukav, in *The Seat of the Soul*, aptly states that we are at a pivotal point in our evolution, which includes choosing whether to align our ego with the soul or not, and this choice must be made again and again. Each choice bringing our egos and souls into alignment causing us to be closer to unfathomable love (Zukav, 2007). He further states that as we align our personality or ego with our soul, we are able to feel unconditional love here on earth (Zukav, 2007).

Action #19: Be Okay with Imperfection

Feeling Authentic Love consistently is not common; it is possible but unusual. As human beings, lapsing into negative emotions is normal. Perfection of

> The perfect you is the love within you.
>
> — *A Return to Love* by Marianne Williamson

continually living with positive emotions is therefore not possible and luckily not necessary to generate Authentic Love. Do not be hard on yourself if negative emotions happen or creep in; love yourself as you would love the most important person in your life, no matter what your thoughts are.

Do not be concerned if you had a negative thought. Authentic Love does not punish, nor is it resentful. It is not conditional. Like the sun, Authentic Love does not just shine on those who appear to deserve it. Authentic Love shines on both the saint and the criminal.

Be soft, caring, and compassionate with yourself when you have negative emotions. It is all part of our existence and learning experiences. Having more compassion for our imperfections will only bring us closer to Authentic Love, as compassion and other positive emotions are paths to Authentic Love.

Action #20: Call upon a Higher Power

For those who feel the need to believe in a power that is greater than we are, one way to come to Authentic Love is to ask for it. Like prayer, asking is a way to receive the answer. In order to receive, we must surrender our faith in that someone or something and believe that they can answer and provide a response to whatever we are asking for.

For others, our higher power may be our higher selves. It

is our soul or higher self that is connected to the Divine that we ask to and receive from. The answers to our questions can come in many forms, including teachers, gurus, friends, enemies, strangers, feelings or voices during meditation, and even songs. It is up to us to be open to receive them; however, the answer comes to us.

You can also call upon a higher power to not only help you realize Authentic Love but the attain the conditions for Authentic Love. That is, one can ask for help in removing the negative thoughts and emotions and fostering positive thoughts and emotions.

When a situation is not going well or did not go well, then recognize that you had some responsibility and were not feeling Authentic Love at that time. You were feeling, for example, anger, selfishness, superiority, inferiority, or another negative emotion.. Then acknowledge this and request a change to make a shift from the negative emotion to Authentic Love, or at least ask to see things differently.

An example of putting this into practice transpired when my friend Amy realized that no matter what her father said or did, she would have feelings of anger. During meditation, she asked why she was feeling this way. She came to recognize that the anger she was feeling toward her father was related to neglect in her childhood. She then came to understand that her father did the best he could with what he knew and that he was a human being deserving of love. So, anytime Amy felt anger arise, she would remember these two points and asked the Divine for help to release her anger and replace it with Authentic Love. It took time, but eventually her anger stopped erupting. Sometimes it still happens, but she sees it, recognizes it, and asks for its release.

Action #21: Believe

If you believe Authentic Love is everywhere, it is everywhere. If you believe Authentic Love is nowhere, Authentic Love is nowhere. If you believe you have Authentic Love, you have Authentic Love. If you think Authentic Love is not for you, Authentic Love is not for you. Believe that what you think you become.

Action #22: Recognize the Ego and What It Is Doing

As noted several times, one of the main reasons we can't feel Authentic Love is because the ego is kidnapping and hijacking our minds, which is covering up our souls. It is obscuring our hearts with fearful, selfish, and self-serving thoughts.

It is a misconception that the mind, and therefore the ego, thinks for and by itself. In actuality, you have control and freedom to think what you want. The ego can put up resistance and find many other ways of staying in control and keeping you in fear. My ego can be very tricky and convinces me that I am being "spiritual" when in fact I am being judgmental.

Actions #3: Managing Negative Emotions and #16: Do What Makes You Feel Good above and Actions #24: Let Go of the Past and #26: Release Judgment of Others and Self below discuss what the ego is actually doing. It keeps you out of the present moment, tricks you into thinking what is good for you when it is not, plays with your emotions, resulting in confusion, wants some things to be different when they can't be, and causes you to act selfishly, to judge, and to feel separate. Your ego can keep you in the past and hanging onto past hurts. The ego also tells us falsehoods, including:

- You do not deserve love.
- You can't feel love because your heart may get broken.
- You will be taken advantage of.
- You need love from someone else as opposed to yourself.
- Falling in love will make you whole.
- Finding a partner will make you complete.
- You are all separate beings.

Do any of these sound familiar?

By recognizing what the ego is doing, you are deflating its power. By reducing ego's power and control over you, it allows the soul to shine through and Authentic Love to be experienced. In actuality, when pain is felt, it is the ego that is feeling this, which is denying Authentic Love.

Action #23: Emulate Great Teachers

We all admire and look up to great teachers such as Jesus, Buddha, Muhammad, Gandhi, His Holiness the Dalai Lama, and Mother Theresa, for example. These were people who exemplified Authentic Love and, as such, were selfless, compassionate, and joyful beings. Nevertheless, we are all made up of the same material that great teachers and enlightened masters are made of. Buddha actually explained that he was an ordinary man that through insight became all-knowing. Marianne Williamson states this so appropriately in *A Return to Love*. She writes that enlightened people, like Jesus, have perfect love inside and nothing else. She further states that we have this potential, this Christ-mind, just as Jesus did, but we are tempted to deny it (Williamson, 1996).

One way to become who they became is to emulate them.

When faced with a situation, ask yourself, "What would Jesus (or Buddha or Gandhi, etc.) do?" It will bring you to a place of non-judgment, patience, and Authentic Love. If you are unaware of what they would do, study them. Read about their lives and read stories about them. Learn what they taught. You will soon get a feeling for who they were and how they led their lives.

Alternatively, there are numerous great living teachers in every religion and spiritual traditions and even wonderful beings who did not follow any tradition, to learn from that are alive today. They are all accessible to those who ask. Follow and take teachings from these great living masters. Soon you will see how they, too, live their lives and emulate them. The great thing about these living masters is that you can always ask them what they would do in specific situations.

Action #24: Let Go of the Past

Hanging on to past hurts and past situations is another way the ego covers up Authentic Love. By keeping you in the past, it keeps you from living in the present and experiencing forgiveness, joy, and peace. The past is not where Authentic Love lives; it is only available in the present moment.

In fact, the past does not exist. It exists as a memory in your mind, taking up the present time, making the present inaccessible. Negative thoughts or negative emotions resulting from reminiscing or ruminating about the past bring you further away from the present and, therefore, Authentic Love. Similarly, even positive thoughts of the past are taking up the present moment and feelings of Authentic Love. However, positive thoughts of the past can put you in a good frame of mind, which can be used to generate positive thoughts when bringing yourself back into the present moment.

There are two ways of letting go of the past, depending if you are reflecting on negative or positive aspects of the past. If you are reflecting on the negative thoughts of the past, you must practice forgiveness. Letting go of the past is directly related to forgiveness, of yourself for your actions and others for their actions. Action #4: Practice Forgiveness provides the procedures for achieving forgiveness.

If you are reflecting on positive aspects of the past, a concerted effort to bring your thoughts into the present moment is needed. As stated in Action #5: Presence and Attention Are Needed, this can be done by remembering to ask the following question throughout the day: "Am I in the present moment?" The question itself transports you into the present moment because the question is being asked in the present, and the present is where you need to be to figure out where your thoughts are. Eventually, the mind is trained to be in the present moment more often, which is where Authentic Love is experienced.

Action #25: Understand Your Inner State

Understanding your inner state is another way of knowing your soul. Your soul is what is left when the ego is subdued, what is the real you, what carries on after death and what is connected to

> Our internal state determines our experience of our lives; our experiences do not determine our internal state.
>
> —*A Return to Love* by Marianne Williamson

the Divine. When you actually come to realize this, Authentic Love will flow.

You also need to understand that what you think and feel, you become. Therefore, if you are angry, you will experience anger. If you are joyful, you will have joyful experiences. You need to take the time on a regular basis and ask the question,

"How do I really feel?" Then you need to ask, "Why do I feel this way?" At times when I check in and ask how I feel, I feel anxiety or that something is not right. When nothing immediately comes to me, I review what happened throughout the day. During this review, I inevitably figure out what I was concerned about, which can range from making a mistake at work to realizing that I forgot to pay a bill. I then let it go or act accordingly. What I have done is understand my inner state on a regular basis to clear out what is keeping me from Authentic Love.

We need to learn that nothing out there affects our inner state. It is how we interpret what is happening out there that affects our inner state. After we have deciphered what our inner state is and why we feel this way, how we deal with this information is the next important step. If we hang on to, stew over, forgive, release, judge, or feel other emotions, this affects our inner state. We are responsible for our internal environment. No one else is responsible.

When I perceive others have negatively affected me, whether I have been betrayed or cut off in traffic, it helps me to decide whether I want to blame and subsequently feel the guilt of blaming or realize that they too are divine, allowing me to forgive and let go. By focusing on the beauty of their souls and freeing any expectations of perfection by others, I am able to release their actions from impacting my inner state. It doesn't mean that I have to condone their actions toward me; it just means that I am not letting them affect me.

Action #26: Release Judgment of Others and Self

Judgment of self and others is a way of fostering negativity. Similar to other negative thoughts outlined in previous chapters, we need to release judgment of others in order to have room for Authentic Love.

So, what is judging? Judging is the act of making assumptions about a person or their actions

> Unconditional love is possible when we reserve judgment of that person.
>
> — Tara Brach

for the purpose of criticizing and justifying. Underlying judgment is the ego's need to prove superiority over the person you are judging. It can also involve the feelings of disdain and disparagement. Essentially, the ego wants to be better than other people and it accomplishes this by focusing on and making the other person less than what the ego sees itself as. This further reinforces its selfishness by putting attention on itself and its desires. The purpose of judging is also fulfilling the need of the ego to understand the other person, whether the ego is right or wrong. The need to understand is based on ego needs and wants, not the soul's aspirations. The soul lets things be as they are with the comprehension that the way people act is based on their own egos or souls. The soul knows that it does not need to know the reason for other people's actions.

However, as human beings, we do need, in many circumstances, to understand others for practical reasons to assist in good relationships. This is considered to be discernment, which includes, for example, understanding another's point of view in relationships and business. Discernment is the act of understanding with judgment.

The ego's purpose of judging itself is similar to judging others. Judging oneself is the ego's attempt at keeping you and your thoughts either in negativity or just engaged, which keeps the ego in control and the focus of your attention. Although judging oneself is different from judging others because the ego is sabotaging you from becoming who you really are and from being who your soul is. All the reasons for judging others and yourself are destructive and therefore act as barriers to Authentic Love.

To release judgment, it is helpful to think that we don't know what causes someone to act the way they do, and we will never know. However, most of what people do is out of fear.

> We love purely when we release other people to be who they are.
>
> —*A Return to Love* by Marianne Williamson

When someone is angry or mean, they are actually acting out of fear ... fear of being hurt and subsequently the need to protect themselves. Knowing that people act out of fear, that you don't know why they do things, and that they are just trying to get through life in search of happiness, just like the rest of us, typically brings out compassion in us. The compassion then leads to Authentic Love, resulting in the release of judgment of others and even ourselves.

Furthermore, when you release judgment of others, you allow people to be who they are. If you have the desire to want someone to be who they are and accept who they are, this can then allow Authentic Love to be experienced. If we let people be who they are, that is Authentic Love.

Action #27: Recognize a Closed Heart

Some people can only accept certain amounts or levels of Authentic Love, dependent on how open their heart is. You may have the experience of giving someone Authentic Love, but they do not return it, they do not recognize it, and/or they do not understand it. Some people do not react or react positively when you send them Authentic Love. They don't take it in because they can't. They are not at or on a vibration where it can be brought in entirely or even partially. We need to love these people anyway, for both our sake and theirs. If they can only take in 5 percent make sure you give them 100 percent because you never know when they will take in 100 percent.

A person who appears to hurt others has a closed heart. By hurting people, they are trying to close others' hearts. This is typically not done intentionally; nevertheless, the result depends on the reaction of the recipient. The reaction of the recipient of the hurt will determine if hurt is actually felt by them. If the recipient feels anger or resentment, then the recipient's heart will be closed, and hurt will be felt. If the recipient can keep their heart open and not be taken in by negative emotions, then they will stay in Authentic Love, and hurt will not be felt. It is our own denial of Authentic Love that causes our own hurt. Therefore, when we recognize a closed heart, it is an opportunity to practice keeping our heart open.

Action #28: Just Do It

Many of us have a fear of saying, "I love you." Growing up, these three words were not used in my home. It wasn't until my twenties that I overcame the fear and told my parents that I loved them. It didn't take long for them to say it in return, which had a huge positive effect on our relationships. I had to release the fear that I was going to be hurt by opening up. Hurt does not happen if we have an open heart. Just do it. Just say those three most important words in our vocabulary. See how it changes your life.

Action #29: Acceptance

Accepting what is actually going on, as opposed to wanting things to be different, is another way to an open heart.

Wanting something or someone to be different is not being in the present moment, as in the present moment, something or someone is as they are. Therefore, wanting it or them to be different takes you out of the present moment, which keeps you from feeling Authentic Love. It also adds conditions to your love, which is not Authentic Love either. In addition, a sense of freedom and liberation comes from accepting things and people as they are. When in a state of Authentic Love, one accepts what is—what is happening and who someone is.

Accepting doesn't mean you like it or that you condone what is going on, if the action is objectionable. All it means is that you accept it for what it is. Furthermore, it doesn't mean that you won't act on it. It means you are aligning yourself with life, not opposing it. You are aligning with the Divine; you are aligning with Authentic Love. This also allows you to accept others and therefore have Authentic Love for them.

In order to accept, we must be able to recognize when we are accepting or rejecting. We need to become aware of our inner state and understand what our ego is up to, as outlined in Action #25: Understand Your Inner State and Action #22: Recognize the Ego and What It Is Doing respectively. When we do this, we will be able to recognize when we are accepting and not accepting what is, thereby liberating us to have more causes and conditions to feel Authentic Love.

Action #30: Give up Limitations

If we have limiting factors to having and giving Authentic Love, Authentic Love will not occur. By stating that I will only feel Authentic Love if she/he does this, if the world is like this, or if this happens, you are limiting the openness of what you will feel. You can learn to keep your heart open as long as there are no limitations.

In order to do this, it is necessary to figure out what closes your heart. For me, there are various situations that result in my heart closing. For example, when someone is speaking out of turn or if someone is expressing negativity, I feel my judgment start, and my heart closes. I say to myself, "Let this pass right through me. It is not actually harming me. Stay open." You must find what dialogue or positive rationale works for you. Eventually, with practice, it will become easier and easier until you heart just stays open.

Action #31: Know Your Intentions

> Love does not obey our expectations; it obeys our intentions.
>
> — Lloyd Strom

Your intentions behind your actions and toward people will either assist or hinder your ability to generate Authentic Love. Positive, helpful, and noble intentions help generate Authentic Love. Similar to adverse emotions, negative intentions will deter feelings of Authentic Love. Even though outcomes of your words and actions are out of our control, even if the outcome or someone's reaction is not positive, your good intentions will support your development of Authentic Love.

To understand your intent, it is comparable to understanding your emotions as identified in Action #1: Know Your Emotions. You need to take the time to ask, "What are my intentions?" Are your intentions to dominate and be right, or empower and nurture? Positive intentions will contribute to your ability to produce Authentic Love.

Action #32: Have Gratitude

Gratitude for all that you have, who you are, what has occurred in your life, and who is in your life is essential for Authentic Love. Gratitude puts you in a positive mind frame, opens and uplifts the heart and is contagious. Being grateful allows more things to come in to be grateful for. When you are grateful, you are more joyous, and when you are more joyous, you have a greater capacity to generate Authentic Love.

I practice gratitude every morning by writing at least ten things that I am grateful for that occurred the previous day. I write about what I am thankful for, which includes what happened that day, who was in my life, the information that I received, and the things that I have, such as my healthy body, my eyesight, and even my car. Start by making the conscious effort to either think or write the things that you are grateful for every day.

Action #33: Practice, Practice, Practice

Once you start generating Authentic Love, it becomes easier, and you will want to do it again and again. The more you practice, the easier it gets. The following are four exercises that you can do to actively generate Authentic Love.

Exercise 1

In order to generate Authentic Love, complete the following exercise:

1. Pick someone that you have positive feelings (e.g., compassion) for, someone you are close to or who has treated you well. This might be a child, spouse, parent, teacher, grandparent, or friend.

2. If you cannot find a person, choose a pet or dream of the type of person you would have positive feelings for (e.g., Jesus , Buddha, or Muhammad).
3. Focus your heart on this being.
4. Release all thoughts and judgments.
5. Feel what you want for that being. This could be gratitude, compassion, love, end of suffering, or peace.
6. Soon you will feel pressure or warm feeling in your heart area but not a negative, painful ache, or you will feel peace come over you. It will be a consuming feeling of just wanting what is best for the being regardless of everything else.
7. Now you are feeling Authentic Love.

Start this process again with someone whom you have neutral feelings for. Then someone you have negative feelings for. It is easier to generate Authentic Love when you are happy and life is going well and meeting your expectations. So, when practicing this exercise on someone you have negative feelings for, it may be best that you are in a good frame of mind. However, the real growth happens when Authentic Love is generated when things are not going well and are challenging.

When I first started on this path, I did not have a child, and admittedly, I did not have strong feelings for my parents. So, in order to focus on generating Authentic Love, I chose an anonymous child that I did not know but was in sorrow, suffering, and did not have the love of a parent.

Then I started doing this exercise in business meetings with someone across the table. In this example, I was able to do this exercise within seconds, and therefore I was able to keep track of the meeting. I subsequently started doing this with strangers—just someone that I saw in the mall or that I saw at a stoplight. This feeling of Authentic Love soon became a state that I felt regularly, since I practiced it regularly.

Exercise 2

Alternatively, instead of practicing on a person, remember a time when you felt Authentic Love. Remember when you felt love for someone that was liberating, without conditions, and made you feel content and at peace. Keep remembering and generating this feeling and the conditions that caused it. Meditating on remembering this feeling can also help transport it into your heart.

Exercise 3

Another exercise to generate Authentic Love is thinking of holding a beautiful baby and the Authentic Love you feel for that baby. Think about how you are going to instill Authentic Love throughout that child's life and nurture the baby, giving the baby all the Authentic Love she or he will need to be a peaceful, confident, courageous, balanced child. Now, think that baby is you. Feel this for yourself.

Exercise 4

Generating Authentic Love can be done through the simplest of gestures. By smiling at someone, making eye contact when listening, cooking and creating, holding the hand of a loved one, laughing and singing. Authentic Love is shown through consideration, smiles, politeness, and attention. Just do these and see how you feel.

The world is healed one loving thought at a time.
—*A Return to Love* by Marianne Williamson

7. HOW DO YOU KNOW IF YOU HAVE AUTHENTIC LOVE OR NOT?

Love is always in you.
—Thich Nhat Hanh

How do you know if you have Authentic Love or not? First answer is: you will know. In case you are still wondering, ask yourself the following questions:

1. Do I feel content, calmly happy, and at peace when I have the feeling that I think is or is related to Authentic Love?
2. Is my intent to nurture and empower the person I am feeling Authentic Love for?
3. Do I feel any negative emotions when I have the feeling I think is or is related to Authentic Love?
4. When I want to say, "I love you," is there something more? Is there a feeling of "I love you if ..." or "I love you but ..."?
5. Is my intent to control, fulfill a need, fill a void, or because I have a fear of being alone?

To answer these questions, you need to know: how you feel, if your ego or soul is answering, and your intentions. If you are having difficulty relating to these three requirements, refer to Action #1: Know Your Emotions, Action #22: Recognize the Ego and What It Is Doing, and Action #31: Know your Intentions. If you can honestly, without doubt, answer "yes" to the first two questions and "no" to the remaining questions, you have Authentic Love. Otherwise, you need to practice the actions more to assist you in generating Authentic Love.

It is difficult to put to words what it feels like to experience Authentic Love. Our language is deficient in this regard. The best way to describe it is when you have several feelings together. These are joy, acceptance, peace, contentment, bliss, calmness, and gratitude. There is a warmth and peacefulness that feels like everything is okay, that you wish all beings the best. There can even be a sense of no other, that you and everyone are one. This feeling of oneness is the ultimate feeling of Authentic Love. When you have oneness, this means that you are no longer identified with the ego but with your higher self, universal consciousness, the Divine, or however or whatever else you identify with as your true nature.

Authentic Love is not typically felt on a consistent basis. Therefore, if one moment you feel what you think is Authentic Love and then something makes you angry, the moment of feeling angry does not take away from the reality that you did feel Authentic Love. Authentic Love starts in moments and grows from there.

Buddha said, "What you think you become." Many other spiritual masters know and teach that you are what you think. If you think you don't have Authentic Love, then you don't. Likewise, if you think you are and have Authentic Love, you are and you have Authentic Love.

If you are still questioning whether you can generate Authentic Love or not, don't worry. Feeling Authentic Love consistently or regularly can take some time. In many cases, you are feeling Authentic Love but you just can't relate the feeling to the term. Intention, consciousness, and practice are what it takes for you to generate Authentic Love more regularly and to identify that it is Authentic Love. Every human being has the capacity to generate Authentic Love. This ability is proven by science and supported by spiritual and religious teachings.

Trust and believe and open your heart. It will come.

Have faith that the Divine is there underlying everything and inspiring us to show Authentic Love.

8. HOW DO I KNOW IF SOMEONE IS SENDING ME AUTHENTIC LOVE?

> **Giving opens the way for receiving.**
> —*The Game of Life and How to Play It*
> by Florence Scovel Shinn

IF YOU CAN INTUIT that you are receiving a love that is unconditional, not controlling, with the best intentions, and if in turn you feel peaceful and content, then someone is sending you Authentic Love. However, intuiting someone else feeling Authentic Love and sending it to us can be challenging. Understanding what someone else is conveying is very difficult, as our history and past experiences can cloud what we see and feel from others. We may have experienced a parent who was passive/aggressive and who smiled during aggressive behavior. Therefore, we may perceive a smiling person as someone who is not necessarily happy.

Our feelings do not lie. But again, we have to be clear on what we are feeling. When we are around someone, if we truly feel that we are at peace, content, and loved without conditions, and their behavior is one of caring and support, then someone is sending us Authentic Love.

Authentic Love does not have to come from those that are supposed to love us (e.g., mother, father, child, husband, wife, etc.). It can come from an acquaintance, coworker, friend, boss, doctor, and so on. It often takes the form of attention or a smile. It can be that simple. There are those people who are able to generate Authentic Love on a regular basis and send it to others. There are also people on this earth, highly realized beings, who have Authentic Love for everyone.

Pure love is a willingness to give without a thought of receiving anything in return.
—*Peace Pilgrim: Her Life and Works in Her Own Words* by Peace Pilgrim

9. HOW DO I FEEL AUTHENTIC LOVE TOWARD THOSE WHO HURT OTHERS?

Love is the only force capable of transforming an enemy into a friend.
—Martin Luther King

EVERYONE IS INHERENTLY GOOD. They may do selfish and mean things, but this is due to the fears of the ego and the notion that we are separate. Everyone has a soul, and the soul is Authentic Love.

When you know someone is inherently good, you can more easily have compassion for them. When they are doing something wrong, you need to recognize that they are harming themselves and others without really understanding that their ego has taken over. Compassion is generated as you acknowledge that they do not understand the truth of their actions. As an example, compassion can be felt for a child learning societal norms like patience and respect. However, this same notion needs to be and can be felt for anyone in the throes of ignorance and bad behavior. You can have compassion for them because of their ignorance, for not understanding the truth of their fears and why they act the way they do.

When a person feels separate, they feel they can act positively or negatively and not be concerned about the implication of their actions on others. This is why so many people hurt others, and since they don't see our oneness, they are actually hurting themselves. Compassion, when you pair it with the understanding that we are all connected and are all one, turns into Authentic Love.

Authentic Love is liberating; it frees one's soul and transcends the trappings of the ego.

10. HOW DO WE TEACH OR HELP OTHERS TO FEEL AUTHENTIC LOVE?

The best way to teach love is to be love.

THE CHALLENGE IS to feel Authentic Love in a world where Authentic Love is not honored, not discussed, and not commonly known. Many people's lives are without love. Many people don't even know what they are missing. They are depressed, angry, and anxiety ridden. They don't know why, and they don't know what to do about it. If people would understand the power of Authentic Love, realize that this is what they are looking for, and work to generate and express it, their lives would be much better, guaranteed.

If individuals felt better, imagine how our communities and countries would feel and benefit. There would be no wars because we wouldn't feel fear. Hunger and poverty would disappear because if we have Authentic Love for everyone, we would do anything to support them. The environment would be healthy because we would realize that the environment sustains us, and if we loved ourselves, we would make sure our support network is healthy as well. In short, the world would be a different place if we expressed more Authentic Love.

Children who do not experience Authentic Love inevitably grow up experiencing emotional difficulties. They have not been taught, felt, or seen by example how to generate Authentic Love within themselves, for themselves, and for others. These children need to learn, talk about, and experience Authentic Love. They need to know what it is and what is missing inside them. They need to know how to generate Authentic Love.

To have more Authentic Love in the world, we must work on ourselves to do what is necessary to reveal Authentic Love. We cannot make anyone else feel Authentic Love and therefore, like most successful teachings and teachers, we need to lead by example. If adults did not exemplify Authentic Love, children would not be able to see and experience Authentic Love and then mimic them. Those adults that have Authentic Love, even intermittently, must show and teach. In order to help others feel Authentic Love, we also need to discuss Authentic Love. For this very reason, we need to dialogue with everyone at all ages. Furthermore, we need to take Authentic Love seriously, not as a romantic notion.

Our education system is a mechanism to teach Authentic Love. Throughout history, many people have been opposed to teaching subjects, like sex education, in schools. They feel these topics are the responsibility of the family and church. However, our educational institutions have evolved to bring issues and topics out of segregation and into schools. Topics have included sex, drugs, racism, abuse, religion, healthy and unhealthy relationships, self-confidence, compassion, violence, war, and a wide range of emotions, including anger and jealousy. As an example, in the 1980s, support teaching sex education increased, primarily due to increase in teen pregnancy and AIDs, and as result, sex education has been part of the standard curriculum. The last and the most important thing that is not taught in schools is Authentic Love. It is time.

Just like sex education was brought into the school system due to significant societal concerns and issues, Authentic Love should be taught in the education system. With the many debilitating psychological issues that are related to the lack of generating or receiving Authentic Love, such as depression and anxiety, this should be a call to action -- the need to educate children on Authentic Love. Doing this would be a departure from the current way of the world. What important concepts weren't?

There are so many of us who have grown up without Authentic Love. Should we just wait and see how things turn out, which is what is happening now, or should we have this discussion with children at an appropriate age? Let's not wait until it is too late as these children grow, have children themselves, and repeat the pattern. They do not know how to give Authentic Love, nor do they know the implications a lack of Authentic Love has on their lives or the lives of their children.

If we do not feel lovable, we won't receive Authentic Love, nor will we be able to generative Authentic Love. The feeling of being lovable typically is typically dependent on being loved as a child. When we are young, we are open and malleable and if we are not loved, we will have difficulty feeling that we are lovable. We will, subsequently, have difficulty showing others love. We need to foster children to feel loved and lovable. If we did not know or feel Authentic Love in childhood, which happens to so many of us, how are we going to be open to let it in when and if it is shown to us as we grow into adulthood? Authentic Love could just pass us by if we are not able to recognize it.

In cases where Authentic Love was not present in childhood, we will not be able to know, accept, or trust any kind of love, even Authentic Love, because it is foreign. In cases where there is abuse in childhood, this can result in not trusting anyone, even if they come with Authentic Love. Even worse, when Authentic Love is given in adulthood, the receiver may then perceive it as negative or feel degraded or even feel abused. Yet, some of these children will grow up desperate for Authentic Love. Desperation can clearly have negative consequences with looking for love in the wrong places. Furthermore, indifference from parents in childhood can be very painful, resulting in low self-esteem or feelings of being worthless.

Feeling Authentic Love as a child provides a foundation for relationships and feelings of self-worth. If you then have experience generating and receiving Authentic Love, you will be able to recognize it. Those who have no experience with Authentic Love assume any type of love or attention is what they are looking for because they have no familiarity with what they actually need or what they are truly looking for.

In order to grow into Authentic Love, we need to debunk some of the negative aspects about love that we have been taught. These include, for example:

- Love fills a void.
- Love is given only if it is deserved.
- Love hurts.
- You should hate and/or be leery of people you do not know or who are your perceived enemies.
- If you are not loved, you are not lovable or worthy of love.

These statements and sentiments are not true, and we therefore need to show and teach the opposite.

There are several positive teachings, such as compassion,

tolerance, and respect, that are taught in schools. This is a good start. We just need to expand this into all of the other aspects of Authentic Love. We should teach, for example, the following fundamental and guiding principles and questions to bring us to Authentic Love:

- Self-love is essential.
- Always ask yourself, what is the most loving thing I can do in the moment?
- Is your love given freely?
- Start loving something that is simple and is not going to be threatening or harm you emotionally, such as nature, a kitten, a puppy, your mother or your father.
- Learn to forgive.
- Start loving someone close to you and then expand this feeling to a friend, then an enemy or someone who has done you wrong, then to someone/anyone on the other side of the world.

Some reading this book may feel like a few of these principles about Authentic Love are too esoteric, that school boards and decision makers will think these principles are too farfetched or not correct and that Authentic Love is just a romantic notion. They feel this way because of their limited understanding of this spiritual path to be taught in school.

However, there are some irrefutable principles that many decision makers will hopefully agree with. These are:

- Authentic Love is a feeling that is needed in our lives.
- Many children (even adults) do not have a healthy understanding of what Authentic Love is.

- Without Authentic Love in our lives, emotional problems are inevitable.

Furthermore, Authentic Love is more than just a spiritual teaching; it is necessary for our survival and to have a good quality of life. We can't leave it up to religions to teach when not everyone seeks religion for answers. Authentic Love and the discussion of Authentic Love need to be part of our everyday lives. Children can't always go to church or seek out spiritual teachers, and parents cannot always be counted on to educate their children. A great percentage of children in our world are required or have the ability to go to school and therefore, the education system is the perfect mechanism to teach children Authentic Love.

Developing and understanding Authentic Love should be our primary purpose to bring up emotionally stable and happy children. It should be our prime focus to dispel hatred, war, jealousy, anger, discontentment, sadness, fear, and lack of confidence. Authentic Love does conquer all. Children only need a few impressionable examples to receive the appropriate knowledge to then move forward in a positive direction of Authentic Love.

What we instill in our children will be the foundation upon which they build their futures.
—Steve Maraboli

11. AUTHENTIC LOVE
 STORIES

Someone who does not run toward the allure of love walks a road where nothing lives.
—Rumi

TRUE STORIES PROVIDE a means of relating to others and learning from others experiences. You may find that these stories are similar to yours and then be able figure out your Authentic Love history. If this history causes you sadness, turmoil, anger, or other negative emotions, you need to take the time to understand it, forgive, and let it go. It is not to hold onto your lack of Authentic Love story as a crutch but to understand, release, and move forward. Stories are also a way of providing inspiration. What people have done, overcome, and grown into gives us the perception that we have that potential and strength as well.

There are millions of stories of people giving, feeling, and receiving Authentic Love. Everyone at some point in their lives has either felt it or received it. We may or may not generate it all the time, or we may have only felt it once and acted on it; however, that is the basis for so many insightful stories. The following are just a few of them. Some are simple one-time events, and others involve a lifetime, but all are profound and extremely beautiful.

a. Josephine's Story

This is a story that my friend Josephine conveyed to me. It shows the process she went through to come to Authentic Love.

Josephine was born to a middle-class family in Canada. As a child, she never remembered being hugged or shown any form of love or attention, with the exception of being kissed on the forehead most nights as she went to bed. She remembered her mother would ask how her day went, but she never felt that she was actually listened to. She was never told that she mattered. She was never asked her opinion. She never felt that her parents every really paid attention to her. She wasn't told that she was important or beautiful. She wasn't asked what she wanted. She wasn't asked what she wanted out of life or if she was happy. Josephine wasn't told, "I love you," until she said it to her parents in her twenties. These are clearly all examples of behavior that would make a child feel that they did not have Authentic Love. Her parents were too involved in their own lives of making money to make ends meet and dealing with their own inner and outer issues to pay attention to her.

Her father was not emotionally available. When he was not at work, he was reading by himself, never really engaging. Her mother was an extremely hard worker, and when she was not working, she was taking courses to better her life. They both were very unhappy in their relationship and therefore could not send Josephine or her siblings joy or Authentic Love. Josephine often speculated that they themselves did not receive Authentic Love from their parents, so how could they give to her what they didn't have or know?

Growing up, she remembers trying to get attention, in particular from her siblings, because her parents were not emotionally available. Sometimes this attention seeking was bothersome and her siblings made it clear that they did not want to have anything to do with her. At times when her siblings and Josephine would fight, Josephine would get spanked or strapped by her father. This was particularly difficult and emotionally traumatic for her.

Furthermore, since Josephine never felt Authentic Love directed toward her, she was not able to give Authentic Love. She didn't know how and didn't know that it existed. However, she does remember that when she was around eleven years old, her family got a dog, and it was then that she started feeling Authentic Love toward her dog, even though she did not know it at the time.

Her parents divorced when she was twelve years old, but nothing changed in terms of her relationships with her family. Her father was still not emotionally available even though they spent weekends together, and her mother was too busy making a living and dating. Even as a teenager, she did not experience Authentic Love from or to a parent or person.

Upon further reflection, her parents may have had Authentic Love for her; however, because she didn't know what it was, she was unable to recognize it. Her parents were not obvious in their love for her. Explicitness is what we need for others to learn and understand what Authentic Love is and why we need it.

During her twenties and early thirties, Josephine was searching for something, as she felt that something was missing from her life. Like most young women who do not know Authentic Love, she searched for romantic love. Her pursuit also took the form of looking for something in spiritual teachings, by reading books on Taoism, Buddhism, Hinduism, and Western spiritual teachers. With only feeling love superficially and yet still sporadically, the process to know Authentic Love was not easy. There was no guidebook or even the words or definitions to help along the way.

When Josephine was thirty-two years old, she married a very kind man that she did have love for, but it was not Authentic Love. Her love was conditional, and since she did not know that her problems were due to a lack of Authentic Love in childhood, she had, during this relationship, a lot of sadness and resentment. Authentic Love between two individuals who know what Authentic Love is, is rare. A relationship in which Authentic Love and romantic love can exist typically requires consciousness.

When she was thirty-three years old, she had a daughter. Then she knew what Authentic Love was. It was a conscious realization of the feeling of Authentic Love. This realization led her to understand Authentic Love.

During her thirties and early forties, Josephine had a lot of anger toward her parents. Through extensive work examining her emotions and feelings, she came to the realization that she did not receive the Authentic Love from her family that she now gives her daughter. She could not understand how anyone could not give Authentic Love to their child. Her anger was directed toward her parents, as she did not receive the Authentic Love that she felt she should have. As a result of this and during this time in her life, she went through a lot of emotional difficulties. She felt unloved, unwanted, and kept regressing back to the child who was lonely, unworthy, and so sad.

Josephine's story has a happy ending. When she finally figured out why she was angry at her family, she began to forgive—forgive her family, for she knew now that her family did not have Authentic Love for her as they did not have it themselves. She also forgave herself for her behavior toward her family during these difficult times. She now has a wonderful Authentic Love relationship for her family.

Josephine's story is typical of many people. Although sometimes a lack of love comes with harshness and violence, and sometimes it is calmly pervasive and everything in between. While her life has been an interesting ride and has brought her to this place, nobody needs to go through the pain of not receiving or giving Authentic Love.

b. Coach

While sitting in my car, listening to the Canadian Broadcasting Corporation, I heard the story of a man named Coach. He was so moved by the turmoil in the Middle East and what the children had been going through in this region that he wanted to bring some joy to the children. He stopped his life in North America and travelled to the Middle East to show children his magic tricks to give them some enjoyment. That is Authentic Love.

c. Mary Johnson and Oshea Isreal

In 1993, Mary Johnson lost her son, Laramiun Byrd, in a gang-related incident. The young man who took his life, Oshea Isreal, was arrested. When he was only sixteen years old, he was tried as an adult, convicted of second-degree murder, and sentenced to twenty-five years in prison. During the trial, Mary gave an impactful statement in which she addressed Oshea. She knew she must forgive him and she told him so, but she also wanted him locked up in prison to pay the cost of killing her son.

The pain and turmoil Mary endured over losing her son was indescribable. Yet she explained that it was like a tsunami, wave after wave of grief and suffering. She also recognized the hatred she felt for Oshea. After many years of self-examination and being active in her church, in 2004 her pastor asked her to teach a class on forgiveness. During the time she was teaching the class, she heard the words that she needed to repent. She needed to repent for the things she had said and thought about Oshea. Then she was told to pray for Oshea like she prayed for herself.

Mary heeded those words and prayed for Oshea and repented for the feelings she had for him. During this time, she matured and took responsibility for her thoughts and actions. She felt that she had actually forgiven Oshea. To prove to herself that she had forgiven him and that the hatred had left her, in 2005 she asked to have a meeting with Oshea.

In 2005, Mary and Oshea met face-to-face. Oshea noticed that when Mary entered the room, there was peace. Oshea admitted to Mary what he had done, and he noticed that Mary asked him a lot of questions about himself, which made him feel like she wanted to get to know him. Mary told Oshea that from the bottom of her heart, she forgave him. Oshea was taken aback and couldn't understand how she could forgive him. At the end of the meeting, Oshea asked Mary if he could give her a hug, and she acquiesced. Mary remembered falling into his arms to the point where Oshea had to hold her up. She felt all the hatred and bitterness leave her.

In 2010, Oshea was released from prison, and Mary held a homecoming party for him. Oshea was startled because the people at the party only knew him for killing Mary's son, but they hugged him anyway. Today, Oshea and Mary live next door to each other, and they speak all over the United States about forgiveness and its power and freedom.

Mary exemplifies not only forgiveness but also Authentic Love. Mary's path, in this situation, to Authentic Love was forgiveness. Mary clearly has unconditional and selfless love for Oshea that is not attached to whether Oshea feels the same. But what also makes this story special is that Oshea also has Authentic Love, in particular for Mary as well as for himself. The impetus for Oshea's Authentic Love for Mary was gratitude. Amongst other things, Mary's forgiveness was probably instrumental in Oshea's forgiveness of himself. Without self-forgiveness, he would not have been able to have Authentic Love for himself.

d. Brenda

Back in 2015, I heard the story of Brenda. One day, Brenda, her husband, and three children went to McDonald's. As they were lining up to get their meal, Brenda noticed the people around her separate and back away. Before she could do the same thing, she realized that there were two homeless men moving forward. Not wanting to be rude and noticing the wonderful smile on one of the men, she didn't move like all the other people did.

The smiling homeless man gave a greeting to her as he held some coins in his hand. The young lady behind the counter asked the men what they would like. The first homeless man replied that he only wanted coffee.

When it was Brenda's turn, she ordered for her family and added two breakfast sandwiches. She walked over to the men and gave them the sandwiches. In doing this, she placed her hand on the first homeless man's hands. With tears in his eyes, he gave her thanks. With tears in her eyes, she walked back to

her family. Brenda said that she learned unconditional acceptance that morning. Brenda experienced Authentic Love in
that moment and also when she shares her story.

e. People of Medicine Hat, Alberta

Medicine Hat is a town in Alberta with a population of about
60,000 people. In 2009, the mayor and council approved the
implementation of House First. House First's mandate was to
eliminate homelessness by 2015. The premise of House First
was based on a study that showed that people cannot stop
taking drugs, get a job, or deal with mental health issues while
living on the streets. It was found that having a home was
essential to overcoming these difficulties.

The goal of House First is that within ten days of realizing
that a person doesn't have a place to live, they will find one.
Medicine Hat was successful in meeting its goal and ending
chronic homelessness. One story is of a man who insisted on
sleeping under cars. They searched for him and kept bringing
him back to his apartment, seventy-five times. It took until the
seventy-fifth try for him to stay in his own home.

The decision makers and supporters of this program
clearly have Authentic Love for the homeless. It shows that
they have no judgment or disdain for people going through
difficulties and that these people just need support. That is
Authentic Love.

f. Dog Story

Not only are humans capable of Authentic Love, so are other
animals. There are many stories of dogs, lions, and gorillas
exhibiting Authentic Love. One story takes place in Argentina
and is of a dog named Captain. In 2006, Captain's owner died,

and the dog went searching for his owner. Eventually, the family found the dog lying on Captain's owner's grave. He returns to the grave every day at 6:00 p.m. to sleep.

This example shows Authentic Love regardless of time, space, comfort, or even presence of the being that one has Authentic Love for.

g. Marc and Mandy Seymour

Not only is this story about the Authentic Love that Marc and Mandy Seymour have for their daughter, Quinn, but it is also about the Authentic Love of a community for Marc, Mandy, and their family. In 2011, Mandy gave birth to a beautiful baby girl. Shortly after her birth, she was diagnosed with junctional epidermolysis bullosa, which is a disease of the mucous membranes, and children typically do not live past the age of one.

Learning of a clinical trial, they moved from Ohio to Minnesota, but unfortunately, Quinn died in 2012. They had been asked if they wished this had never happened. Their answer was no. They did wish that their daughter had been born perfect and was still alive, but they said that this experience gave them a beautiful gift—that true love does exist in our world. These two people generated Authentic Love under an extremely difficult situation, which is even more amazing. They were able to have Authentic Love for the daughter regardless of the conditions, without attachment to situation or outcomes, selflessly and obviously without their egos in the forefront.

During this time, Marc started blogging about their experience, and he had 10,000 followers from all over the world. Marc said that he felt unconditional love from all of these people—family, friends, and strangers. The community got together and held benefits for them to help with the financial support they needed when the insurance company would not cover all expenses. Authentic Love came to Marc and Mandy because they had Authentic Love.

h. People of Possom Trot, Texas

The people of Possom Trot, Texas, a town of six hundred people, have adopted seventy-six children, and almost all have graduated from high school. This story began with Donna Martin and her husband who is a preacher at Bennett Chapel. During a time of great turmoil after her mother died, Donna was remembering the special unconditional love she felt from her mother. She received a message from God, who asked what it would be like for children who did not receive this mother's love. God wanted Donna to give children this love, which is clearly Authentic Love.

When Donna and her sister, Diann, started the process of adopting from foster care, they were told that these children had been abused and didn't trust or understand love. Diann was the first to adopt, and the community could clearly see the Authentic Love and joy she had for her four-year-old adopted son and the love her adopted son had for her. This love soon became contagious. She actually told the community that the boy was hers and that they should adopt as well ... and they did.

With the many issues they came across with their children who were working through psychological problems like trust, all of the parents supported and cared for one another. Clearly, these foster parents were exhibiting Authentic Love for these children and for each other through their attention and support. How else could they get through these difficult times if the love wasn't unconditional and selfless? Authentic

Love resulted in stable children who finished high school and went on to further education, jobs, or their own families, even though their initial upbringing was devoid of Authentic Love.

i. Sereno

Sereno is a horse that lives in Brazil. His thirty-four-year owner died unexpectedly, and knowing how close Sereno was to his owner, his owner's brother brought Sereno to his funeral. When the casket approached, the horse walked up and sniffed the coffin. He then laid his head down on the coffin. During the funeral procession, the horse whimpered and stomped his feet. Everyone at the funeral felt that the horse was mourning the death of his beloved owner. The love shown by Sereno exemplifies Authentic Love. All sentient beings can experience Authentic Love.

j. Grant

Grant is a boy who loves life, plays musical instruments, has a purple belt in karate, and loves to dance. This seven-year-old boy has dwarfism and has been ridiculed, called a baby, and been stared at, yet he has incredible wisdom and Authentic Love. He has been quoted as saying, "My wish for the world is that everyone can love one another. Even if they fight. Sometimes ... just love one another. No matter what troubles there are in the world, we'll be happy as long as there's love. What if people look different than you? Should you still love them? Yes, you should. Because everyone is just a loving person. It doesn't matter whether you're short or tall, or black or white ... We're all just people doing our very best."

Let us dream of tomorrow where we can truly love
from the soul,
and know love as the ultimate truth at the heart of
all creation.

—Michael Jackson

AFTERWORD

This book was the result of insight received during meditation and insight received at the strangest of times (e.g., in the shower, while driving, during quiet contemplation and writing in my gratitude journal). It was also the result of receiving wisdom from teachers in my life, in particular, my Buddhist teacher, Lama Lhanang Rinpoche. It was also the result of having my son, Conner. Without him, my path to Authentic Love would have been so much more difficult. He made it so easy to have Authentic Love for him, just because he came into my life.

It was also the result of many years of contemplation. Trying to understand why I was angry with my parents, trying to understand why I was always searching, trying to understand why I always felt something was missing, and trying to understand why I got so upset when relationships ended. Eventually, it resulted in understanding, receiving, and generating Authentic Love and feeling contentment with myself.

Understanding Authentic Love has become my mission in life. I have spent large amounts of time meditating, reflecting, reading, and comprehending what is going on in my life and others' lives. Once I understood what Authentic Love was and the necessity of Authentic Love to survive and flourish, life has been clear and full of joy. Not knowing Authentic Love is what stood in my way of experiencing real happiness, living in the moment, feeling fulfilled, and loving anyone, including myself. I now know that Authentic Love is a requirement in life and needs to be discussed and acknowledged.

ABOUT THE AUTHOR

Kimberley Arnold was born and grew up in Toronto, Canada. She obtained her bachelor of science degree from the University of Guelph in 1989 and her Master's of environmental studies from York University in 1994. While she has spent most of her adult life working as an environmental consultant and an artist, understanding why she is here in this existence has been her life's passion and quest. From a young age, she asked this question, which led her to study Taoism and then Tibetan Buddhism. Kimberley studied and practiced under Lama Lhanang Rinpoche and received numerous teachings and empowerments from great Tibetan masters, including His Holiness Penor Rinpoche and His Holiness the Dalai Lama. Tibetan Buddhism has had a great impact on Kimberley's understanding of her existence through teachings on compassion, loving kindness, equanimity, and emptiness, to name a few. Through these teachings and with the benefits of meditation, Kimberley began to know her own heart and the ultimate realization of love, Authentic Love.

More recently, Kimberley studied books by great Western spiritual teachers, including Louise Hay, Wayne Dwyer, Marianne Williamson, Gary Zukav, Eckhart Tolle, and Deepak Chopra. All of these teachers have provided insight into her understanding of Authentic Love. Through the teachings and guidance of great spiritual teachers, Kimberley has received the clarity of her understanding of life as outlined in this book.

Kimberley is also a Celtic artist, and love has played a central role in all of her Celtic art pieces. Kimberley currently lives on Cape Breton where she continues to write and do Celtic art.

Her website is www.kimberleyarnold.com.

BIBLIOGRAPHY

Abdu'l-Baha. Tablets of Abdu'l-Baha v3 – Abdu'l-Baha. 1909. *Tablets of Abdul-Baha Abbas*, 524–526. Chicago: Baha'I Publishing Committee.

Ainsworth, MDS. 1967. *Infancy in Uganda: Infant care and the growth of love.* Baltimore: Johns Hopkins University Press.

Bernard, Bonnie. "Fostering Resilience in Children." *ERIC Digest* (1995).

Bowlby, John. 1951. *Maternal Care and Mental Health*. The Master Work series (2nd ed.). Northvale, NJ, London: Jason Aronson. ISBN 1-56821-757-9. OCLC 33105354. Geneva, World Health Organization, Monograph series no. 3.

Bowlby, John. "The Nature of the Child's Tie to His Mother." *International Journal of Psycho-Analysis* (1958): 39: 350-373.

Bowlby, John. "Separation Anxiety." *International Journal of Psycho-Analysis* (1959): 41: 1-25.

Bowlby, John. 1960. "Grief and Mourning in Infancy and Early Childhood." *The Psychoanalytic Study of the Child* (1960): 15: 9-52.

Byrne, Rhonda. 2006. *The Secret*. New York: Atria Books.

Canfield, Jack. 2005. *The Success Principles*. New York: HarperCollins.

Chopra, Deepak. 1998. *The Path to Love: Spiritual Strategies for Healing*. New York: Three Rivers Press.

Emoto, Masaru. 2001. *Hidden Messages in Water*. New York: Atria Books.

Farley, R. Chris & Phillip Shaver. "Adult romantic attachment: theoretical developments, emerging controversies, and unanswered questions." *Review of General Psychology* (2000): 4: 132-154.

Field, Tiffany M. (Ed.). 1995. *Touch in Early Development*. New Jersey: Lawrence Erlbaum Associates Inc.

Harlow, Harry. "The development of affectional patterns in infant monkeys." In *Determinants of Infant Behaviour,* edited by B. M. Foss, 15: 307. Oxford: Wiley, 1961.

Hay, Louise, 1991. *The Power is Within You*. Carlsbad, California: Hay House, Inc.

Hay, Louise. 1999. *You Can Heal Your Life*. Carlsbad, California: Hay House, Inc.

Hazan, Cindy & Phillip Shaver. "Romantic love conceptualized as an attachment process." *Journal of Personality and Social Psychology* (1987): 52(3): 511-524.

His Holiness the Dalai Lama. 2000. *The Little Book of Buddhism*. London: Rider Books.

Lake, Gina. 2006. *Radiance*. Endless Satsang Foundation.

Lewis, Thomas, Fari Amini & Richard Lannon. 2000. *A General Theory of Love*. New York: Random House.

Luby, Joan. "Maternal support in early childhood predicts larger hippocampal volumes at school age." *Proceedings of the National Academy of Science* (2012): 109: 2854-2859, doi: 10.1073/pnas 1118003109

Moorjani, Anita. 2012. *Dying to Be Me*. Carlsbad, California: Hay House Inc.

Nyanaponika Thera. "The Four Sublime States: Contemplations on Love, Compassion, Sympathetic Joy and Equanimity. *"Access to Insight (Legacy Edition),* November 30, 2013, http://www.accesstoinsight.org/lib/authors/nyanaponika/wheel006.html

Pinker, Steven. 2011. *The Better Angels of Our Nature: Why Violence Has Declined*. New York: Viking Books.

Rein, Glen. "Effect of Conscious Intention on Human DNA." *Proceeds of the International Forum on New Science* (1996): 1-12.

Rohner, Ronald. "Transnational Relations Between Perceived Parental Acceptance and Personality Dispositions of Children and Adults: A Meta-Analytic Review." *Personality and Psychological Study Review* (2012): 16: 103-115, doi 10.1177/1088868311418986.

Rose, Mark Alton. 2005. *Especially for Christians: Powerful Thought-provoking Words from the Past*. New York: Iuniverse Inc.

Singer, Michael. 2007. *The Untethered Soul: The Journey Beyond Yourself*. Oakland: New Harbinger Publications, Inc.

Pendleton, Linda. 2003. *A Small Drop of Ink: A Collection of Inspirational and Moving Quotations of the Ages*. New York: Iuniverse Inc.

Smith, Peter. 1999. *A Concise Encyclopedia of the Bhah'I Faith*. Oxford: Oneworld Publications.

Schucman, Helen. 2007. *A Course in Miracles*. Omaha: Course in Miracles Society

Thich Nhat Hanh. 1987. *Old Path, White Clouds: Walking in the Footsteps of the Buddha*. Berkeley: Parallax Press.

Thubten Chodron. 2012. *Don't Believe Everything You Think: Living with Wisdom and Compassion*. Boston: Shambhala Publications, Inc.

Williamson, Marianne. 1996. *A Return to Love: Reflection on the Principles of A Course in Miracles*. New York: HarperCollins.

Zak, Paul J. 2012. *The Moral Molecule: The Source of Love and Prosperity*. New York: Dutton.

Zukav, Gary. 2007. *The Seat of the Soul*. New York: Simon & Schuster.

Zukav, Gary. 2008. *Soul to Soul*. New York: Free Press.

RECOMMENDED READING

Byrne, Rhonda—*The Secret*

Chopra, Deepak—*The Path to Love*

Hay, Louise—*The Power Is within You*

Hay, Louise—*You Can Heal Your Life*

Lake, Gina—*Radiance*

Moorjani, Anita—*Dying to Be Me*

Singer, Michael—*Untethered Soul*

Williamson, Marianne—*A Return to Love*

Zukav, Gary—*Seat of the Soul*

Zukav, Gary—*Soul to Soul*

NOTES

3. Why Do We Need Authentic Love?

1. As quoted in *A Small Drop of Ink: A Collection of Inspirational and Moving Quotations of the Ages* (2003) by Linda Pendleton.
2. As quoted in *Especially for Christians: Powerful Thought-provoking Words from the Past* (2005) by Mark Alton Rose.

4. What Happens When I Have Authentic Love?

1. As quoted from Mata Amritanandamayi's website: http://amma.org/about/how-she-began.